At Issue

Has Child Behavior Worsened?

Other Books in the At Issue Series:

Age of Consent
Animal Experimentation
Are Abortion Rights Threatened?
Are Unions Still Relevant?
Child Pornography
The Children of Undocumented Immigrants
Club Drugs
Designer Babies
Do Cell Phones Cause Cancer?
Do Infectious Diseases Pose a Threat?
Embryonic and Adult Stem Cells
Extending the Human Lifespan
High School Dropouts
Is Foreign Aid Necessary?
Is Selling Body Parts Ethical?
Reality TV
Should Drilling Be Allowed in the Arctic National Wildlife Refuge?
Technology and the Cloud
Teen Residential Treatment Programs
What Is the Future of the Music Industry?
What Is the Impact of Digitizing Books?
What Is the Impact of Twitter?

At Issue

Has Child Behavior Worsened?

Amy Francis, Book Editor

GREENHAVEN PRESS
A part of Gale, Cengage Learning

Detroit • New York • San Francisco • New Haven, Conn • Waterville, Maine • London

Elizabeth Des Chenes, *Director, Content Strategy*
Cynthia Sanner, *Publisher*
Douglas Dentino, *Manager, New Product*

For more information, contact:
Greenhaven Press
27500 Drake Rd.
Farmington Hills, MI 48331-3535
Or you can visit our Internet site at gale.cengage.com

LIBRARY OF CONGRESS CATALOGING-IN-PUBLICATION DATA

Has child behavior worsened? / Amy Francis, Book Editor.
pages cm. -- (At issue)
Includes bibliographical references and index.
ISBN 978-0-7377-6834-3 (hardcover) -- ISBN 978-0-7377-6835-0 (pbk.)
1. Social interaction in children. 2. Social interaction in adolescence. 3. Children--Conduct of life. 4. Youth--Conduct of life. 5. Child psychology. I. Francis, Amy.
HQ784.S56H37 2014
302.5083--dc23

2013024571

Printed in the United States of America
1 2 3 4 5 6 7 15 14 13

Contents

Introduction

According to the US Centers for Disease Control and Prevention, approximately 9.5 percent of children aged four to seventeen (5.4 million) were diagnosed with ADHD, or attention deficit hyperactivity disorder, as of 2007. This marked an increase of 22 percent from 2003 to 2007. Why the rate of ADHD cases increased so dramatically is a matter of intense debate. While many believe increased awareness is helping identify more cases, critics argue that parents or teachers seek the diagnosis as a means of obtaining medication to control difficult children.

Dr. Dathan Paterno is among those who are critical of the diagnosis. He writes on his blog, "ADHD is *not* a real disease. It is *not* a neurological disorder. . . . ADHD is simply a description for a list of behaviors that are annoying to parents and teachers and for which they currently do not know how to effect change." He is not alone in this belief that ADHD is primarily a behavioral issue.

Psychologist L. Alan Sroufe wrote on January 28, 2012, in the *New York Times*, "Behavior problems in children have many possible sources. Among them are family stresses like domestic violence, lack of social support from friends or relatives, chaotic living situations, including frequent moves, and, especially, patterns of parental intrusiveness that involve stimulation for which the baby is not prepared." He concludes, "Putting children on drugs does nothing to change the conditions that derail their development in the first place."

While MacLean Gander, writing for *USA Today*, December 8, 2012, agrees that the increase in diagnosis is unwarranted, he believes parents and teachers have little choice but to seek the diagnosis in order to hit high-achievement benchmarks. For this he blames the 2001 No Child Left Behind federal legislation, which tied school funding to student performance and created a situation in which school systems are "less hospitable to students with certain learning profiles." "Teachers," he writes, "under pressure to guide their classes to high-performance on standardized tests, can control the classroom more effectively if they can recommend that high-energy students be controlled through medication." Gander is further concerned that if students continue to be diagnosed with ADHD at the current rate, more than one in five will be classified as such and receiving medication within the next couple of decades.

Many other researchers, physicians, and parents, however, firmly believe ADHD is not only real but is underdiagnosed and undertreated. They argue that children who do not receive the appropriate diagnosis and treatment for their ADHD not only suffer academically but also receive the constant message from adults that they are bad kids because of their inability to control their behavior. Dr. Tanya E. Froehlich, a developmental and behavioral pediatrician at Cincinnati Children's Hospital Medical Center, warned in a September 4, 2007, *Washington Post* article that untreated ADHD can lead to "lower rates of school and career achievement and higher rates of substance abuse, incarceration, injuries and car accidents."

As for parents seeking an ADHD diagnosis to medicate their children as a means of controlling their behavior, a 2006 study by researchers at Washington University School of Medicine in St. Louis suggests that is not true. The researchers found that nearly half of the kids with an ADHD diagnosis are not receiving treatment for the disorder. Dr. Richard D. Todd, as quoted in *ScienceDaily* on August 6, 2006, states, "Only about 58 percent of boys and about 45 percent of girls who had a diagnosis of full-scale ADHD got any medication at all." The article states that the bigger problem may be that while we are getting better at diagnosing the disorder, parents are still reluctant to medicate their children.

According to another study from AboutOurKids.org, a resource of the New York University Child Study Center, girls have the hardest time getting the diagnosis and related treatment. The study states, "Boys with ADHD are usually easy to spot because of their behavior. . . . Girls are more likely to have the attentional type of ADHD, which can lead to difficulty in attending and focusing rather than in disruptive behavior. . . . Most of the research has been done with boys, and as many as 50 to 75 percent of girls with ADHD are missed."

Dr. Manuel Mota-Castillo is less worried about underdiagnosing children with ADHD than he is about misdiagnosing and overlooking more serious mental health disorders. In a July 1, 2007, *Psychiatric Times* article, he stated that he was concerned with the "terrible consequences that often follow when a disorder is incorrectly diagnosed and treated in emotionally disturbed young people." For these children, the medications most frequently given for ADHD can exacerbate their symptoms. He described one young patient who experienced "hallucinations, racing thoughts, insomnia, elevated mood, and grandiose ideation" after receiving stimulant medication for her supposed ADHD. He further writes:

> "Hyperactivity," "oppositional behavior," and "defiance" may be seen in a variety of neuropsychiatric disorders. This does not mean that we should ignore better-defined disorders such as bipolar disorder and reflexively diagnose ADHD or ODD [Oppositional Defiance Disorder]. . . . Both diagnoses may open the door to blaming the victim for behavior that he or she cannot control and denying medical services to patients in desperate need of psychiatric services.

The diagnosis and treatment of ADHD, particularly as it relates to behavior, will no doubt be hotly debated for years to come. This and related questions about child behavior are explored at length by the authors of the viewpoints in the following pages of *At Issue: Has Child Behavior Worsened?*

1

Classroom Behavior Has Worsened

Frank Schultz

Frank Schultz is the education and politics writer for the Janesville Gazette *in Janesville, Wisconsin.*

The last few decades have seen an increase in the number of children with behavior problems in the classroom. This is challenging for everyone involved—teachers, parents, and children. Possible reasons for the decline in good behavior may include lack of good parenting, increased use of technology, parental substance abuse, dietary changes, and the economy. Positive behavior programs have grown in popularity and are seeing some success, and recognizing and treating mental illness in children earlier may also prove to be part of the solution.

A girl told her mother a kid poked her in the tummy with a pencil, causing a bruise. Then it happened again the next day.

Four or five kids in a class of about 22 were running around uncontrolled, slamming doors and pushing other kids, parent Diane Mayhew said.

A boy was seen poking his hand up a girl's skirt. The same boy held scissors to the necks of his classmates, one witness told Janesville [WI] police.

All of the above were kindergartners at Janesville's Van Buren Elementary School earlier this year [2012].

Frank Schultz, "Children Behaving Badly: Has it Gotten Worse?" *Janesville Gazette GazetteXtra*, April 29, 2012.

"It's to the point where these children are hazards to other kids and the teacher," Mayhew said at the time.

Mayhew, who also has a boy in high school, said it wasn't like this when he was in kindergarten.

Some teachers agreed, off the record, that the number of problem children has increased in recent decades, and the problems are showing up in increasingly younger children, making teaching a tougher job.

The extent of children with problem behaviors is hard to gauge. Clearly, there still are plenty of children who behave well at school.

Parental Frustration over Problem Behavior in the Classroom

Mayhew was one of several parents with children in the same class who complained to *The [Janesville] Gazette* after becoming frustrated with the school's responses.

Parent Heather Kemps said her daughter was punched in the face and hit in the head with a wooden block, causing bruising and swelling.

"My son complains lot about having headaches every day because of screaming and yelling," said parent Jamie Chareumthasouk. "He told me his friends say 'F' word and the 'B' word."

Mayhew met with her child's teacher, the principal and the superintendent. She was assured steps were being taken, but she was not told what. School officials won't reveal those details because of laws that ban disclosure of identities of students with disabilities or who are disciplined.

But the teacher at Van Buren hinted at a problem in a letter to parents obtained by *The Gazette*: "Some of the children are struggling with following directions and practicing safe classroom behavior. We are also stressing the importance of using appropriate language in the classroom. Please talk to your child every day.... Encourage your child to tell you if they have had any issues with other children. Please notify me if your child ever mentions getting hurt or inappropriate behaviors."

District Superintendent Karen Schulte acknowledged the classroom has problems, but she said they were being addressed. The school's building coordinator, Stephanie Pajerski, was one of the district's best kindergarten teachers until she was promoted this year to run the school, Schulte said

Pajerski told Schulte some of the kindergartners' behaviors were "challenging" but nothing unusual and nothing Pajerski hadn't seen in her career, Schulte said.

Working in a classroom is more difficult than it was 30 years ago.

"Kindergartners are impulsive and spontaneous on top of that, and rambunctious, so you have to factor that in as well," Schulte said.

Schulte said several times that classroom management is the teacher's responsibility.

"Do we have other challenging classrooms—kindergartens—in the district with even more children? Yes we do. They're running very well," Schulte said.

Schulte said the district brought in experts and pulled one student from the Van Buren classroom. She acknowledged that working in a classroom is more difficult than it was 30 years ago when she first taught.

"We do see an increase in autism, for example, and other behaviors that are much more challenging," Schulte said. ". . . School districts across the nation are identifying more students with behavioral issues than we have in the past."

Roberta Sample has seen many behavior-challenged children over the decades, first as a volunteer and then 12 years as the school district special-education parent liaison.

"Master teachers tell me, 'I don't know what it is, Roberta, but I've never had a first-grader tell me to "F" off before,'" she said.

"They tell me, 'It is different, Roberta. I can't tell you why, but the behaviors and the responses are different.'

"Somebody should listen to them. They've been on the front lines forever."

Identifying the Reasons for the Decline in Good Behavior

Sample resigned in 2010 but stays tuned in to parents and teachers. She believes teaching has gotten harder and children more difficult for a variety of reasons:

"Inept parents" who don't know how to set limits for their children and who apparently think it's OK for kids to learn vulgar language at a young age.

Technology—"At a very young age, they have access to materials that I would've been shocked if my 15-year-old had access to it. We don't supervise because I don't know that we know how to supervise it."

Sample said she is getting more calls from families with children who have accessed "extremely pornographic websites."

Substance abuse—Wisconsin has long been a leader in alcohol abuse, Sample said, and it's known that alcohol affects fetuses. Society has not dealt with that problem as it has done with tobacco, she said.

Sample—not a health-food geek by any means—wonders if chemicals in foods we eat also might affect child behavior.

Mental health problems, often related to drugs and alcohol, which are not treated, sometimes because there's no money.

"As a society, we just need to pick up our own problems and stop saying 'I don't know what to do.' Start somewhere."

Sample said society is to blame for not giving parents the tools they need to bring up their own children.

"You can't just blame families and children, and you can't just blame teachers," Sample said. "It's a shared burden."

Simone DeVore, associate professor and early childhood education coordinator at UW [University of Wisconsin]-Whitewater, said schools have higher academic and behavioral expectations of kindergartners.

"That raises the impression that we have more children with behavior problems. I'm not so sure," DeVore said.

At the same time, teachers are dealing with a rise in autism and with more poverty and more diverse populations. Sometimes it's a problem of understanding the child, DeVore said.

Teachers are dealing with a rise in autism and with more poverty and more diverse populations.

"Every behavior has a function, so teachers need to figure out what the child is trying to tell me, and that requires training, of course," DeVore said.

Demands on teachers to get more training have increased, DeVore said, and luckily, Wisconsin has good professional-development resources.

Families also have more demands on them, and both parents often are working.

"Stressors families experience in the home can very much impact a child's behavior in school," DeVore said. "The function of the behavior is maybe to seek attention."

Rewarding Good Behavior and Other Possible Solutions

Schools say they are addressing discipline problems with programs that are said to be research-based "best practices." The programs, such as PBIS—Positive Behavioral Interventions and Supports—preach a behavioral code and try to steer children to do the right thing by rewarding good behavior.

At Janesville's Roosevelt Elementary School, students who behaved well recently were recognized with a lunch ceremony, a picture display in the office, a certificate and recognition on the school website and in school announcements, according to a recent blog by Schulte.

At Van Buren School, in the same report: "Office discipline referrals are down for the quarter. Students continue to assist with morning announcements by reciting our mission statement and Eagle Expectations, along with sharing personal examples of how they are making positive choices and following our expectations."

Parents with concerns aren't taken as seriously as they should be.

Other programs such as Response to Intervention focus resources on children with the most difficult problems as early as possible so they don't worsen as the child moves through the grades, Schulte said.

"Parents are overworked. People are working two jobs," Sample said. "I can learn more about children by visiting a day care than by talking to Mom and Dad. That's scary,"

Good teachers are coping, but working in a difficult classroom will wear down even the best of teachers, Sample said. She said schools and parents need more common sense.

Sample said the Janesville School District has a culture of insisting the schools always do the right thing, so parents with concerns aren't taken as seriously as they should be.

"You can't say, 'My kid would never do that,' because the minute your child leaves your supervision, they may do whatever they wish," Sample said. "And you can't say, 'My teacher would never say that or do that.'"

Teachers sometimes feel things have gotten much worse, but that could be a narrow view, said Marge Hallenbeck, who retired in 2010 as director of at-risk and multicultural programs in the Janesville district.

"If you have a tough class this year, that's what it looks like, but you tend to forget the good years," Hallenbeck said.

Mental disorders are one reason children might act up at school.

These problems often arise at young ages, but they may not be diagnosed or treated for years, experts said.

One in five children has a mental health disorder, according to the National Center for Children in Poverty, and up to 80 percent of children and youth in need of mental health services do not receive them.

Early treatment is key, experts agree.

The problem of early mental disorders is just beginning to be recognized, and too often children are not treated until long after problems arise, said Simone DeVore, early childhood education coordinator at UW-Whitewater.

A recent survey showed that psychiatric hospitalization rates have increased for children ages 5 to 12, rising from 155 per 100,000 children in 1996 to 283 per 100,000 children in 2007. The increase was the greatest among all age groups, said Lana Nenide of the Wisconsin Alliance for Infant Mental Health.

The use of anti-psychotic medications in children is on the rise as well.

"Helping children as early as possible is very important. The longer we wait, the more behaviors become entrenched," Nenide said. "In fact, research shows that when aggressive and antisocial behavior has persisted to age 9, further intervention has a poor chance of success."

"We must work on prevention and early intervention," Nenide added. "When we wait, we might be too late."

2

Misbehavior at School Is Normal

Yasmine Phillips

Yasmine Phillips is an education reporter for Australia's Herald Sun *newspaper.*

Children are nicer now than in the past. However, when a child does misbehave at school, parents need to realize that this is part of learning, too. Instead, parents too often get defensive and blame the school, other students, or point to a child's diagnosis. Parents would do better to simply accept that children will misbehave at school and support the school when it happens.

The head of WA [Western Australia]'s peak group for primary principals has issued an unexpected message to parents, saying schools expected children to make mistakes.

But WA Primary Principals Association president Steve Breen said some parents were increasingly defensive of their child's misbehaviour, and more likely to point the finger at the school or blame bullying.

Problem Parents

"There is a general lack of risk taking by a lot of children because they are protected or there is a protection veil over them," he said.

Yasmine Phillips, "Parents Need to 'Chill Out' and Accept Children Will Misbehave at School," *Herald Sun*, November 3, 2012.

"They are supposed to get dirty, they're supposed to have a little fight, they're supposed to have disagreements, they're supposed to get angry and they're supposed to cry. That's part of growing up.

"All children tell untruths and schools are not upset about that because everyone does it—and it's part of life. But when a parent is questioned about a child making an untruth, they will not believe the school, they will believe their child.

"I think a lot of people don't realise that schools are extremely socially minded. We expect children to make mistakes, we expect children to be naughty—but a lot of parents get very defensive if their child has been accused of something by another parent or from another child.

"Don't worry about it. Chill out. It's all part of growing up. I ask parents about what they did in primary school and they'll tell you all the terrible things they did and I say: 'Well why don't you let your child do that?'"

Mr Breen said 90 per cent of parents did the right thing, but many had become over-protective to the point where children were less open to taking risks—and therefore learning important lessons.

Many parents blamed their child's misbehaviour on Oppositional Defiant Disorder, a behavioural problem characterised by disobedience and hostility, or bullying.

"A parent will drive one street to school with their child in the back, drop them off and then drive one street back," he said.

"There's other incidents where they're very protective about when they're in other people's care but not necessarily when they're in their own care.

"Basically children—if they're very protected, they don't want to take a risk and learning is all about taking risks. A child mightn't jump off the little playground because they've been told not to when it's perfectly OK or if it's too high they will never do it again. You can't tell a kid that—they have to actually learn that."

Blaming Oppositional Defiant Disorder

A school principal, who did not want to be named, said many parents blamed their child's misbehaviour on Oppositional Defiant Disorder [ODD], a behavioural problem characterised by disobedience and hostility, or bullying.

While they said most of today's children were nicer than they've ever been, the principal said "so many parents will now question the word of the school when very mature, supportive adults are saying this is what happened".

"There's no doubt about that—that has trampled into schools," they said.

"I've been dealing with a parent today who genuinely believes that none of their children has ever done anything wrong. It's just an automatic fallback that their kid is innocent and the school has made a mistake.

"There's also a connection with ODD—parents love ODD. They say their child has this disorder and the school has to adjust to it. I've been in the game a long time now and I have no doubt there is a condition called ADHD [attention deficit hyperactivity disorder]—the trouble is once a kid believes they've got it and once a parent believes they've got it, it becomes an excuse.

"The relationship between ODD kids and parents who never believe their kid has ever done anything wrong, I believe, is very strong. I think that's the characteristic, rather than the kid having the characteristics."

Australian Medical Association WA psychiatry spokesman Paul Skerritt said ODD was merely a description of certain behaviour, rather than an excuse for poor behaviour. Dr Skerritt said people today were more likely to look for someone else to blame.

"We were expected to fight our own battles, including at school. It was very rare in my day for parents to intervene at all," he said.

"But the blame game is an interesting one. It goes right through to the legal system too. There have been great increases in law suits of people who might have just decided to put up with it years ago. There is quite a bit of that—of looking for someone to blame.

"It's much easier to blame the teacher than yourself—and often blaming yourself is totally unnecessary anyway."

3

Modern Children Lack Basic Manners

The Florida Patriot

The Florida Patriot *is an online political news and commentary publication.*

In the wake of new reports of the severe bullying of a sixty-eight-year-old bus monitor in New York state, parents should consider how they are teaching their own children respect at home. With so many extra demands on teachers these days as well as unreasonable limits that don't allow schools to use effective discipline techniques, parents need to take charge of teaching their children basic manners at home and should be held accountable when children misbehave at school.

Growing up as a child in the 1970's in Miami from the time I can remember I was taught to open doors for ladies and respect my elders. I was not a perfect student and neither were my friends, however, in my whole educational experience I cannot remember anyone ridiculing or disrespecting a teacher, bus monitor or other school employee to their face in a bullying manner especially. As a matter of fact, back in my day we didn't need bus monitors to control school students during the bus ride. This week [June 2012] the especially harsh bullying of 68 year old bus monitor Karen Klein

"Hold Parents Accountable for Their Child's Lack of Manners," *The Florida Patriot*, June 24, 2012.

[in upstate New York] should make a lot of Americans take a very hard look in the mirror when it comes to their parenting skills, and wondering why our country's scores in schools are falling behind.

Stop Blaming Teachers

Far too often, many cable news pundits and politicians want to point a finger at public school teachers and say they are not doing their job. Teachers these days are now responsible for teaching manners, civility, and other things and still find time to teach math, science and don't forget the all important FCAT [Florida Comprehensive Assessment Test]. This reminds me of a time in 6th grade (1980) when three boys were giving a substitute teacher a particularly hard time and the substitute left and came back with our assistant principal. The assistant principal assembled the entire 6th grade and gave 3 paddles a piece to these three boys during the beginning of the year. For the rest of the year I cannot remember a similar incident or problem of this magnitude happening again.

What would happen if John cursed out his teacher and John and a parent had to spend their Saturday cleaning the school/in study hall in the library?

Imagine what would occur if this incident were to happen today? The assistant principal would be criminally charged with assault and battery, the children would be whisked away for psychological counseling, and the parents would hire Gloria Allred [lawyer famous for taking high-profile cases] to sue the school system for multi-millions. We are teaching this generation that they are untouchable, they do not have to be accountable for their actions, and that there are no consequences for their actions. How is a school teacher with 30 or more children supposed to teach biology or algebra with these distractions?

Some say that Private For Profit Charter Schools are the answer to this problem. How many parents are actually sitting at the kitchen table and helping their children with their homework instead of watching *American Idol*? If we take the same kids that aren't being taught manners and move them to a different type school how have we fixed the problem?

Why don't we start holding the parents of the children causing the problems accountable? Currently, John curses out his teacher and gets sent to the principal, given detention, a note to take home, etcetera, and the parent that failed this child is unaffected and the behavior continues. What would happen if John cursed out his teacher and John and a parent had to spend their Saturday cleaning the school/in study hall in the library? Why don't we start a program like this in the elementary schools and I can guarantee you that John's parent/parents are going to get tired of cleaning the school bathrooms/attending study hall on the weekends and this child's behavior would improve. Think of how many young men we could change and give a great education to instead of have them continue on the same way until they drop out and start committing crimes. Let's give the school teachers a hand by making parents be accountable and at the same time give the children who want to learn a chance to without class being disrupted constantly.

4

Today's Teens Are Better Behaved than Their Parents Were

Laura Sessions Stepp

Laura Sessions Stepp is a widely published Pulitzer Prize-winning journalist who writes about the lives and culture of youth.

Despite strong evidence that teenagers are more responsible and have better behavior than previous generations, few adults believe it. The reason may be that adults quickly forget how they behaved as teenagers or they over-generalize from teens they know personally. Additionally, teenagers today who are just entering the workforce now face challenges unknown to older generations. Adults need to have more empathy and less criticism.

Do you think young people today act more or less responsibly than in years past?

If you answer less, you've got a lot of company. Although you'd be wrong on several counts.

In a recent column on CNN.com, I noted that teenagers are not taking as many health risks as they used to, according to a large national study released by the Centers for Disease Control and Prevention. They're smoking less and drinking less, fighting and using firearms less frequently, getting preg-

Laura Sessions Stepp, "Teens Doing Better: Why Don't Adults Believe It?," CNN, April 20, 2011. cnn.com.

nant and giving birth less often. I noted that this is true even as the teenage population has grown in size and diversity.

Adults Don't Buy It

To say that many readers didn't buy it would be an understatement. Many were downright hostile to the notion that young people might actually be faring better than previous generations, including one who said teens are, in fact, "in a worse state than ever."

"Teenagers have a 'lower IQ,'" this reader said, and "the number involved in violence and gang activity is rising. . . ."

Another commenter said teens are "completely incapable of thinking for themselves"; "don't give a crap about anything but themselves"; and have "an appalling lack of any sense of remorse for wrongdoing."

Another opined: "Kids today are . . . becoming the most narcissistic, self-centered yet. They're obsessed with Facebook and looking at pictures of themselves . . . they don't study nearly as much as Asian kids. . . ."

"They all got the tattoos!" yet another said. "And the girls with the tramp stamps and cleavage tats. Who wants to hire them?"

Young people have made significant progress in critical areas. So why does it seem that so many adults are reluctant to believe that young people are more responsible?

As the comments rolled in, the focus shifted to people in their 20s who, the critics said, are unmotivated and unable to make decisions without the help of mom and dad. "It's not the current kids, it's the generation before them," wrote one person. "Far too many are selfish, rude, totally self-absorbed and lazy."

Of course, young people's performance is not improving on all measures. While the proportion of those 25 and older who have at least a college degree is increasing, it lags behind that of other developed countries.

Still, young people have made significant progress in critical areas. So why does it seem that so many adults are reluctant to believe that young people are more responsible? I turned for answers to three professionals who study the younger generation.

Gene Roehlkepartain, vice president of Search Institute, a 53-year-old youth development organization, says people tend to generalize quickly, basing their opinions entirely on their own experiences.

"Everyone knows personally one or more kids whose lives didn't turn out well or that ended tragically," he says. "It's hard to accept a general statement about overall patterns when you have a particular case seared in your memory."

For some, it apparently doesn't matter if that memory is decades old. Said one reader, "These polls are very wrong. I'm 52. My oldest son is 31. By the time he was 14 he had tried every drug and alcohol known to mankind. Had a girl pregnant at 15. . . ."

One thing was clear from the harsher reactions. Older adults tend to forget the beers they consumed when they were young, the classes they skipped, the music they played so loudly that the family dog ran for cover. One fellow writer called other colleagues out on this. They were, the writer said, suffering from AOA, or Adult Onset Amnesia.

Social historian Stephanie Coontz calls it the "fun house mirror effect."

Time modifies memory, says Coontz, author of *A Strange Stirring*, a new book about women of the 1950s and '60s. Hearing about an escapade that a child got into, it's easy to say, "I wasn't like that," just as you would look into a distorted mirror at the carnival that showed you with three heads and say, "That's not me."

Maybe some of these ranting readers have lost their jobs, homes and health insurance. Maybe they're at that stage in life where they suspect they'll never achieve their dreams and resent those who still have dreams.

Coontz says it goes beyond resentment, however. The troubled economy is recovering very slowly, the country is engaged in war overseas and leaders of our two main political parties are at each other's throats more than usual. Such turmoil can lead people to lose hope in their future, she says, and when they do, they also lose hope in their kids.

Including "kids" 18 and older. One commenter, identifying himself as an academic adviser at a Texas university, said that although some young people are all right, most of them have "no common sense and no drive! They can't think or make decisions without calling Mom and Dad. . . ."

Yes, says Richard Settersten, professor of human development at Oregon State University, more young adults are close to their parents, even living at home after high school or college. But if they once felt entitled to an easy life, they no longer do. Many of those staying with their parents are doing so to afford to go to college or, if they're already out of college, pay off debt.

Different Times

In these uncertain times, it's a mistake to believe that the younger generation should think and act like we did, says Settersten, co-author with Barbara E. Ray of a recent book about 20-somethings called *Not Quite Adults*. Companies running smoothly today may be bought out or go bankrupt next year; jobs may change or disappear; health insurance may be affordable one year and not the next year.

As children, today's youth "were told they could be anything and now they're here and they can't," Settersten says.

"The quick start, lock-step life is dead for everybody. Yet we still carry it around in our head as a yardstick for young people."

At least one commenter on the website acknowledged this, reminding other writers that high unemployment affects the youngest members of a work force first. He also noted that the interns where he works "are some of the best I've seen in a long time."

He was not the only contributor who showed an understanding of, and affection for, the younger generation. And although sympathetic writers appeared to be in the minority, I was heartened that their observations drew more "likes" than the remarks that were critical or mean.

I took away one other thing: The sheer volume of comments—about 1,000 within a few days—indicates that no matter what their specific opinion is, people do care about kids. Maybe that's something to build on.

5

Millenials Are More 'Generation Me' than 'Generation We' Study Finds

Joanna Chau

Joanna Chau is a writer, reporter, and multimedia journalist.

Younger Americans are drawn more toward selfish pursuits, such as money, image, and fame, and are less likely than previous generations to be involved in civics, donate to charity, or take action to protect the environment. Although some cite a rise in community involvement among young people as evidence to the contrary, this is mostly due to schools requiring participation and does not reflect a shift in attitude. Individualism is now the norm, and this will have negative effects on our society as a whole.

Millennials, the generation of young Americans born after 1982, may not be the caring, socially conscious environmentalists some have portrayed them to be, according to a study described in the new issue of the *Journal of Personality and Social Psychology*.

The study, which compares the traits of young people in high school and entering college today with those of baby boomers and Gen X'ers at the same age from 1966 to 2009, shows an increasing trend of valuing money, image, and fame more than inherent principles like self-acceptance, affiliation, and community. "The results generally support the 'Generation Me' view of generational differences rather than the 'Gen-

Joanna Chau, "Millennials Are More 'Generation Me' Than 'Generation We' Study Finds," *The Chronicle of Higher Education*, March 15, 2012.

eration We,'" the study's authors write in a report published today, "Generational Differences in Young Adults' Life Goals, Concern for Others, and Civic Orientation."

For example, college students in 1971 ranked the importance of being very well off financially No. 8 in their life goals, but since 1989, they have consistently placed it at the top of the list.

The study—by Jean M. Twenge, a professor at San Diego State University; Elise C. Freeman, a graduate research associate at the same university; and W. Keith Campbell, a professor at University of Georgia—is the latest to seek to define the behavior and traits of the millennial generation.

Young people have been consistently taught to put their own needs first and to focus on feeling good about themselves.

Views on this much-debated topic have varied widely among experts.

In 2000, the popular book *Millennials Rising: The Next Great Generation*, by Neil Howe and William Strauss, portrayed the group as engaged, high-achieving, and confident, among other "core traits."

Ms. Twenge, the lead author of the new study, believes otherwise.

She has also published a book on the millennials, *Generation Me: Why Today's Young Americans Are More Confident, Assertive, Entitled—and More Miserable Than Ever Before*, in which she writes: "I see no evidence that today's young people feel much attachment to duty or to group cohesion. Young people have been consistently taught to put their own needs first and to focus on feeling good about themselves."

That view is apparent in the new study's findings, such as a steep decline in concern for the environment. The study found that three times more millennials than baby boomers said they made no personal effort at all to practice sustainability. Only 51 percent of millennials said they tried to save energy by cutting down on electricity, compared with 68 percent of baby boomers and 60 percent of Gen X'ers.

The study also found a decline in civic interest, such as political participation and trust in government, as well as in concern for others, including charity donations, and in the importance of having a job worthwhile to society.

The millennial generation has been raised in a culture that places "more focus on the self and less focus on the group, society, and community," Ms. Twenge says.

"The aphorisms have shifted to 'believe in yourself' and 'you're special,'" she says. "It emphasizes individualism, and this gets reflected in personality traits and attitudes."

Even community service, the one aspect where millennials' engagement rose, does not seem to stem from genuine altruism. The study attributes that gain to high schools in recent years requiring volunteer hours to graduate. The number of public high schools with organized community-service programs jumped from 9 percent in 1984 to 46 percent in 1999, according to the study.

Most of the study's data point toward more individualism and less cohesion. The advantages of individualism are more tolerance, equality, and less prejudice, says Ms. Twenge. But the broader implication, she says, is not good.

"Having a population that is civically involved, is interested in helping others, and interested in the problems in the nation and the world, are generally good things," she says. But Ms. Twenge does not believe this is happening. People are "more isolated and wrapped up in their own problems," she says. "It doesn't bode well for society in general."

6

Teens Are More Civic-Minded Now than in the Past

Kimberlee Salmond and Judy Schoenberg

Kimberlee Salmond is a senior researcher and Judy Schoenberg is the director of research and outreach at the Girl Scout Research Institute.

In 2009, the Girl Scout Research Institute published a study that indicates that youth today intend to be more involved with charity and to volunteer, vote, and care for the environment more than they did twenty years earlier, when the study was previously conducted. Also, the reasons why they say these things are important have changed since 1989. For example, they are more likely to act, not out of a sense of obligation, but because of a desire to do what is right. Today's youth have a strong moral compass and feel that they have adults in their lives who care about them. More youth today say they would turn to an adult for advice instead of follow what a friend would say than in the past. However, the data show that those concerned more with their own happiness and getting ahead in life are also more likely to engage in risky behaviors, as well as cheat, lie, and cyberbully.

While media portrayals often depict youth as irresponsible, lazy, and morally corrupt, our study offers a different perspective, in which youth are responsible to themselves and others and value being involved in their

Kimberlee Salmond and Judy Schoenberg, "Good Intentions: The Beliefs and Values of Teens and Tweens Today," Girl Scouts of the USA, 2009.

communities. It also sheds light on an emerging generation that in many ways is more committed to these values than were their predecessors 20 years ago.

The major findings of the research are that youth today:

- Say they will make responsible choices and refrain from risky behaviors.
- Value diversity and acceptance.
- Demonstrate a strong sense of civic commitment and engagement.
- Say they can withstand peer pressures and are willing to stand up for themselves.
- Are strongly influenced by parents, families, and religion when confronting moral dilemmas and ethical decisions. As well, youth employ their own moral compasses to make decisions.
- Differ by gender in some attitudes and how they approach certain decisions.

. . . There have been shifts in the kinds of decisions today's youth say they would make compared with youth 20 years ago, such as abstaining from premarital sex, refusing a drink when offered one at a party, telling the truth to the school principal, not cheating on a test, and continuing a friendship with a friend who is gay or lesbian.

More youth today than in 1989 exhibit a commitment to civic responsibility and engagement.

Another prominent change from 20 years ago is the higher percentage of youth today who intend to be civically engaged in their communities. More youth now than in 1989 say they will vote (84% vs. 77%) and give to charity (76% vs. 63%) in the future. As well, this study demonstrates that young people draw significant influence from peers and adults in their lives to make decisions, but at the same time, employ their own moral compasses when doing so.

This report fleshes out the findings stated above and discusses the role that adults have in helping youth actualize their intentions around personal and public responsibility. Youth today say they want to take the responsible road and avoid unhealthy behaviors, but intent and action do not always match. Youth today are also committed to civic engagement through high interest in volunteering and giving back. Overall, young people need meaningful leadership opportunities so they can effect the kind of change they are most interested in—change that makes a difference in the world. . . .

Youth Today Demonstrate a Strong Sense of Civic Engagement

Most youth expect to vote in every election, give regularly to charity, and volunteer in their community. Furthermore, many youth cite being personally motivated to do these things, rather than feeling obligated to do so. More youth today than in 1989 exhibit a commitment to civic responsibility and engagement.

Regardless of age or gender, many youth say that the most important reason for helping people in their community is that it makes them feel good personally (46%). Girls and younger youth are more likely to say this (51% of girls compared to 41% of boys; 50% of 8- to 12-year-olds compared to 42% of 13- to 15-year-olds and 43% of 16- to 17-year-olds).

Voting. The majority (84%) of 7th- to 12th-graders say they intend to vote in every election, up from 77% in 1989. Motivation for voting has shifted in the last 20 years—more preteens and teens today say they will vote because it is personally what they want to do (59% vs. 42% in 1989). A higher percentage of youth in 1989 said they would vote out of obligation—because it's the right thing to do (35% vs. 25% now).

African American (66%) and White (62%) preteens and teens are more likely than their Hispanic (51%) and Asian (45%) counterparts to say that voting in every election is what they personally want to do; Asian (38%) preteens and teens are more likely to say they will do it because it is the right thing to do compared with White (23%) and African American (22%) youth of this age.

Charitable Giving. Today's preteens and teens also plan to be generous. Three-quarters (76%) say they will regularly give to charity, compared to 63% in 1989. Girls plan to give to charity at a higher rate than boys (80% vs. 72%) and are more motivated by feeling it is personally what they want to do (43% vs. 26%).

Nearly 8 in 10 youth today (79%) are interested in volunteering in their immediate community.

Volunteering. Today's youth intend to volunteer locally and nationally. Nearly 8 in 10 youth today (79%) are interested in volunteering in their immediate community (this question was not asked in 1989 so no comparison data are available). As well, 37% of youth say they will volunteer for a year to serve their country in something like AmeriCorps or Peace Corps. This question was asked 20 years ago and the number is similar to what it was then.

Girls (81%) are more likely than boys (77%) to be interested in community volunteering, while more boys (40%) than girls (33%) intend to volunteer as part of a national program.

Military Engagement. An area where youth's interest has dropped in the last 20 years is military engagement. In 1989, 22% of youth in grades 7–12 were willing to fight in a war under any condition, while only 10% say this now. One-third of youth are not willing to fight at all (34% compared to 18% in 1989), with girls significantly more likely than boys (43% vs. 26%) to say this. African American youth (54%) are more likely than those who are White (31%), Hispanic (30%), or Asian (30%) to say they would "fight under no conditions".

Taking Care of the Environment. Youth exhibit a strong sense of community and global responsibility in their attitudes toward environmental stewardship. Fully 78% of 7th- to 12th-graders—girls and boys across all age groups;—agree that everyone has a responsibility to take care of the environment. A higher percentage of Hispanic preteens and teens feel this way (86%), compared to 82% of Asian, 77% of White, and 70% of African American youth.

Overall, today's youth exhibit a strong sense of civic and community responsibility, and in many ways, plan to be more engaged than did youth 20 years ago. . . .

Youth Today Draw Strong Influence from a Variety of Sources

Parents and Families. Parents and families play a large role in the lives of young people today. The vast majority of youth say they have an adult in their life who cares about them (94%), and this percentage is highest for White (95%) and Asian (90%) respondents. Of the youth who have someone who cares, 92% specify their parent(s).

As well, youth have a greater constellation of adults who care about them than they did in 1989. Fully 68% cite a grandparent, uncle, aunt, or other extended family member as a special adult in their lives, compared to 59% who cited this 20 years ago. Youth now are also more likely to say that a teacher or coach is a special adult in their life (44% vs. 33%).

Today, White youth are more likely than African American and Hispanic youth to name a grandparent, uncle, or aunt

(73% vs. 59% vs. 66%); teacher or coach (49% vs. 38% and 37%); neighbor (26% vs. 18% and 16%); or adult leader of a youth group (20% vs. 10% vs. 14%) as someone who cares about them.

The majority of 7th- to 12th-graders (87%) look to their families to help solve America's problems.

Parents are also the most common source of advice (62%) when youth encounter uncertainty in a given situation. This is followed by friends (31%), and a grandparent, uncle, aunt, or other extended family member (a combined 19%). However, turning to parents decreases as youth age. Boys (65%) turn to their parents for advice at a higher rate than do girls (58%), but as they get older both boys and girls decline similarly in how often they say they turn to their parents. In addition, White youth (65%) are more likely to turn to their parents than African American youth (54%).

More girls (39%) than boys (23%) say they turn to friends. As youth get older, friends figure more prominently as a source of advice. White youth (35%) are more likely to turn to their friends than are Hispanic (25%) and African American (22%) youth.

Twenty years ago youth turned to their friends for advice at a higher rate than they do today. In 1989, 43% said they would turn to a friend their age if they didn't know the right thing to do, compared to 31% now.

The majority of 7th- to 12th-graders (87%) look to their families to help solve America's problems as well. This is followed by teachers and educators (85%), and the government (76%). Science and investors are also important, although more boys (70%) than girls (61%) think this. About 6 in 10 (58%) say that neighborhood or community groups play a role. This is particularly true for Asian (67%) and African American (64%) youth. As well, 57% of youth say that religious leaders and organizations have a role, and African American young people are more likely to say this (67%) compared to other racial/ethnic groups. Only 22% look to celebrities to help solve America's problems.

Parenting style also relates to youth's choices. What kind of relationship do parents have with their children? What is most likely to happen when youth and their parents disagree about something? When asked to respond to which parenting style best represents their own experience:

- Forty percent of youth say their parents explain why it is important to act according to their wishes.
- Thirty percent say they decide together with their parents what is best.
- Twenty-two percent say their parents force them to do what they (parents) think is best.
- Five percent say their parents give in and let them do whatever they want.

While this study cannot determine behaviors that are a direct result of parenting style, some interesting distinctions emerge. For example, a higher percentage of youth who say their parents either "give in" or "force" say they would commit behaviors such as cheating and lying, compared to those who say their parents explain decisions or they decide together. Youth with parents who give in are also likely to say they would have sex, drink, and cyberbully.

Moral Compasses. When unsure what to do in a particular situation, youth are also guided by a variety of moral compasses. The following compasses are based on the work of Dr. Robert Coles and were used in the 1989 survey, with the exception of Conscience Follower, which was added due to its popularity as a write-in choice 20 years ago:

- Conscience Follower—24%: Youth follow their conscience/do what they think is right.
- Conventionalist—19%: Youth follow the advice of an authority, such as a parent or teacher.
- Theist—13%: Youth do what God or scripture tells them to do.
- Expressivist—11%: Youth do what makes them personally happy.
- Civic Humanist—8%: Youth do what is best for everyone involved.
- Utilitarian—5%: Youth do what improves their situation or helps them get ahead.

Nine percent of youth answered "don't know" and 11% left this question blank. There are interesting demographic and attitude differences between youth in these categories.

A quarter of youth (24%) follow their conscience, which is particularly true of teenagers. This is the most common moral compass.

Almost 2 in 10 youth (19%) say they follow the advice of an authority figure. Not surprisingly, this group seeks to follow rules and feels more pressure to do so. Younger youth are more likely to say they do this than their older counterparts.

Just 5% of youth make decisions based on their own self-interest in getting ahead.

Thirteen percent of youth say religion is very important in their current and future decision making.

Eleven percent of youth are concerned primarily with their own happiness. These youth feel pressure to engage in riskier behavior and make less responsible choices, and are less likely to value civic engagement.

Eight percent of youth seek to do what is best for everyone involved.

Just 5% of youth make decisions based on their own self-interest in getting ahead.

These moral compasses distinguish youth's responses to the dilemmas presented. Overall, youth who identify as Expressivist ("do what makes you happy") or Utilitarian ("do what improves your situation or gets you ahead") are more likely than others to say they would cheat on a test, lie to a school principal, cyberbully, and have premarital sex. Expressivist youth are the most likely to say they would drink alcohol, and Utilitarian youth are more likely than most others to say they would end a preexisting friendship with a person they learned was gay or lesbian.

Age. As evidenced throughout the text, youth response tends to vary according to age. Overall, younger youth tend to stick to the rules and have a stark sense of right and wrong. As youth get older, they see the world through more nuanced eyes and are more interested in testing boundaries. For example, older youth are more likely to say they will engage in behaviors like drinking and having premarital sex. Attitudes about abortion also change—as youth get older they are more likely to agree that abortion is justifiable.

As well, younger youth are more likely to say they would not cheat on a test and would tell the principal the truth if a friend had destroyed school property.

The moral compasses that youth prefer also vary by age. Those who say they follow their conscience or do what gets them ahead tend to be older than those who say they defer to an authority figure or to the dictates of their religion.

Religion. Other important factors relate to the kinds of decisions youth make, including religious inclination. Seventy-one percent of today's youth say their religious beliefs are important to them, with religion diminishing in importance as youth age. This has remained constant over the last 20 years. More African American youth (88%) say their religious beliefs are important to them than Hispanic (69%), White (68%), and Asian (59%) youth.

Religious youth are less likely than less religious or non-religious youth to say they would lie, cheat, drink, or have sex.

Youth today are intent on making responsible choices, respecting others, and engaging in their communities and civic life.

Youth who are more religious are also less likely to think that smoking, abortion, gay/lesbian relations, and sex before marriage are permissible.

Academic Performance. Another factor in youth's decision making is how well they do in school. In particular, getting high grades or low grades distinguishes approaches to school-related scenarios and risky behaviors. Youth who get low grades are more likely than those who get high grades to say they would cheat on a test (13% vs. 6%), lie to a school principal (34% vs. 23%), drink alcohol (22% vs. 17%), and have premarital sex (35% vs. 25%).

Overall, this research shows that certain factors relate to how youth make decisions, including parenting style, personal moral compasses, religion, school performance, and age. . . .

People often lament the declining moral values of youth. However, this study paints a more encouraging picture: that, generally speaking, youth today are intent on making responsible choices, respecting others, and engaging in their communities and civic life. In several ways, it is youth who are charting a new direction for the country—towards personal and public responsibility.

7

Youth Today Are Really No Different than Previous Generations

Marie Hartwell-Walker

Marie Hartwell-Walker is a psychologist and marriage and family counselor, author of the e-book Tending the Family Heart, *and contributor to Psych Central's "Ask the Therapist" column.*

The latest generation has been unfairly labeled "entitled." There are some in every generation who feel a sense of entitlement, just as there are also some who dedicate their lives to teaching, providing medical care, and volunteering. Each generation attempts to establish their own identity and the generation that comes before reacts with shock and indignation. There is truly very little difference in the mentality of youth between generations.

The word of the year seems to be "entitled." Get a group of older adults together and you'll hear a fair amount of grumbling about the self-centeredness and selfishness of the 20- and 30-somethings. They're the new Me Generation, the kids who have been coddled and spoiled by parents, given trophies for just showing up, and repeatedly told that they are special just the way they are. They question authority, expect rapid promotions, and think they deserve a lot for doing very little. Paradoxically, they also feel that they have a right to stay dependent on aging parents well into their twenties. Right? Wrong. This generation is as diverse as those that came before.

Marie Hartwell-Walker, "What's the Matter with Kids Today?," Psych Central, 2009. http://psychcentral.com/lib/2009/whats-the-matter-with-kids-today.

The current group of 50+ year olds would do well to remember that we were the recipients of similar exasperation from our 50's and 60's parents. Labeled and skewered by [novelist] Tom Wolfe as the occupants of the first "Me Decade" our huge demographic bulge has fascinated and terrified for decades. We came of age in the 1960s and early 1970s. The styles of the times, long hair, short skirts, and refusing to shave (both sexes), scandalized our elders. Music and dance styles made parents roll their eyes and wonder what the world was coming to.

Under that umbrella of prevailing style, however, were enormous differences. Yes, there were those who embraced free love, dropped acid, and dropped out. Others joined in a cult of self-absorption, spending money and time primal screaming, rebirthing, pre-deathing, and encounter grouping in a constant quest for self-actualization.

But there were also those who gave years of their lives to the Peace Corps, Vista Volunteers, and nonprofits. They organized communities and established schools, medical and mental health clinics, and legal services for the poor and disenfranchised. They campaigned for equality among the races and between the sexes. Some fought as honorably as they knew how in the Viet Nam war. Others fought equally honorably against it. To characterize the entire generation as drugged out hippies trailing behind the Grateful Dead or navel-gazers endlessly searching for the "aha" moment of self would do the generation a huge disservice.

Interest in community service through such organizations as the Peace Corps, Volunteers of America, and AmeriCorps is again reaching the high of the '60s.

Whatever the conventional wisdom about the Boomers, as adults we encompass the political far left to the far right; the still pony-tailed human service provider to the buttoned-down corporate executive. We may all remember when the Beatles came to America; we may think of the Frost-Nixon interview as a memory, not a movie; we may have some shared and powerful cultural references, but ultimately the characterization of Boomers as the first generation of "me" doesn't mean much.

Today's Generation Is No Different

Today's generation of young people is no different. Yes, there are those who spend more time in the virtual than the actual world, making relationships with people they will never meet. Others seem addicted to constant background music of their own choosing. Rap makes the music of the Beatles and the Rolling Stones seem like lullabies. Piercings, tattoos, and, shall we say, innovative hair colors and styles scandalize the adults.

Under the umbrella of prevailing style, however, are enormous differences. Yes, there are kids who think they are entitled to get what they want just because they want it. They are the college students who debate their professors' evaluation of lackluster work on the grounds that they "tried hard" or who feel that they deserve a top job despite minimal effort. They are the 20-somethings who are living with their parents because they would rather buy a better car than pay their own rent and whose parents can't seem to find a way to tell them to grow up and get on with life.

But there are also college students who year after year go on "Alternative Spring Break." While some of their peers party on Florida beaches, these kids continue the work to clean up and rebuild cities and towns hit by [2005 Hurricanes] Katrina and Rita. Interest in community service through such organizations as the Peace Corps, Volunteers of America, and AmeriCorps is again reaching the high of the '60s. Young people are volunteering to staff the Special Olympics, to be a Best Buddy, and to clean up the environment. They are signing on to Bill Cosby's Bridges to the Future Project to improve impoverished rural schools. Some fight with conviction and honor in Iraq and Afghanistan. Others fight with equal conviction and honor against those wars. There are young people who work at two and three jobs to put themselves through college, who accept and learn from their teachers' critiques, and who expect to work hard for whatever they get. To characterize the entire generation as entitled and whining about their "Quarterlife Crisis" would do the generation a huge disservice.

Whatever the conventional wisdom about the youth of today, they encompass the political far left to the far right; the tattooed rapper to the computer whizzes of Silicon Valley. 9/11 may be a shared defining event for their generation; they may all know how to simultaneously text, Twitter, and Facebook while plugged into iPods; they may have some shared and powerful cultural references, but ultimately the characterization of the kids of the early 21st century as an entitled generation doesn't mean much.

It's just true that every adolescent group pushes on adult values as a way to establish their own identity. Behavior that shocks and appalls certainly gets the attention of the media and reactions from those of us who make a living commenting on trends. Often, the result is a label that makes for good news and endless analysis but that also overwhelms the reality of diversity.

It also puts the current grownups in the good company of generations of adults who have gone before. Consider this quote from a thinker named Hesiod in the eighth century B.C.: "I see no hope for the future of our people if they are dependent on the frivolous youth of today, for certainly all youth are reckless beyond words. When I was a boy, we were taught to be discreet and respectful of elders, but the present youth are exceedingly wise and impatient of restraint."

Or how about this one, attributed by Plato to Socrates [Greek philosophers] of ancient Greece: "The children now love luxury; they have bad manners, contempt for authority;

they show disrespect for elders and love chatter in place of exercise. Children are now tyrants, not the servants of their households. They no longer rise when elders enter the room. They contradict their parents, chatter before company, gobble up dainties at the table, cross their legs, and tyrannize their teachers."

Like most attempts to characterize a generation, the idea of entitlement may be trendy, and even accurate for some, but the truth is far more complicated. Why can't kids today be more like we were? The answer is simply that they are.

8

Video Games Are Responsible for Increased Youth Violence

Ron Moten

Ron Moten is the cofounder of Peaceoholics, an antigang, antiviolence organization based in Washington, DC.

Violent video games and movies desensitize youths to violence and lead to more violent behavior. Despite some success with efforts to keep violent games out of the hands of young people, the video game lobbyists have prevented any legislation from being passed that would make these efforts more widespread. Legislation must be passed, however, to prevent more needless tragedies.

It was 2005, but I remember it like it was yesterday. Jauhar Abraham, who co-founded Peaceoholics with me, and I were headed to Oak Hill Youth juvenile detention facility to conduct group sessions with troubled youths. When we walked into the facility, we found the teenagers glued to the TV playing "Grand Theft Auto," a video game in which players steal cars and otherwise commit murder and mayhem in huge amounts. Many of these youths wound up where they were for committing crimes very like the ones they were committing in the video game. Needless to say, we were outraged.

The Impact of Violent Media

To find out what kind of impact such games had on them, we held focus groups with the youths. I recall one of them telling me that, before he started playing the games, he would have

Ron Moten, "Violence on the Screen, Violence in the Streets," *The Washington Post*, December 28, 2012.

never gotten into a stolen car, a step which led to stealing cars later on and eventually to violent carjackings—just like in the game. Then one youth I will never forget said that playing the games put him "in a zone" to do what he had to do to survive. This young man would later be killed, and after his death several murders would be attributed to him.

It was obvious that the violent games desensitized these youths to violence. But I didn't really need them to tell me this. The focus groups brought back memories of when I was growing up. I was just as easily influenced by the entertainment industry. Many of my friends either wanted to be like [basketball player] Michael Jordan—or Scarface [a drug lord in a well-known violent film of the same name].

Did we idolize Jordan because he was the most exciting basketball player of all time? Or could it have been because he showed up in pretty much every other commercial on television? Scarface was a different story. Tony Montana—Al Pacino's character in the movie of that name—was admired for how he rose in the drug game. I saw the influence firsthand when some of my friends began saying, "Say hello to my little friend"—Montana's famous line—before committing acts of violence similar to what they saw glorified in the film.

Thousands have fallen victim to assaults, stab wounds and gunshots—all of which our children act out daily in video games that grow more violent all the time.

Abraham and I knew we had to do something with what we were learning about the negative impact of violent media. With the support of civil rights activists, we set out to train youths who were once members of rival gangs to become activists. During our sessions with them, we discussed the impact of violent video games. They came to see themselves as change agents with the power to stop this poison from reaching their peers.

We had some successes with our work and started attracting media attention. Adrian Fenty and Jim Graham took the lead on D.C. Council legislation aimed at stopping violent and sexually explicit games from getting into the hands of minors. But once the powerful lobbyists from the video game industry got involved, it all went nowhere.

Now we have seen the horrific massacre in Newtown, Conn. [in which twenty-six people, mostly children, were killed inside a school in December 2012], and we're having the same conversation all over again. For District [Washington, DC] residents, the violence displayed in Newtown is all too familiar. In 2010, five young people were killed and nine wounded in the South Capitol Street massacre, only a few miles from where our president resides. Data show that murder is down in the District, but this is misleading to some degree. Since 2005, thousands have fallen victim to assaults, stab wounds and gunshots—all of which our children act out daily in video games that grow more violent all the time.

Time for Legislation

And yet some continue to argue that our violence-infested entertainment cannot possibly influence an individual to commit acts of terror. They are wrong.

It's time for the District's legislators to bring back the bill ensuring that parents and merchants are obligated to keep these games out of the hands—and minds—of our children. Additionally, we must ensure that every child in America who needs mental health services gets them, while also stopping them from self-medicating through violent games. Remember, hurt people hurt people. Let's all be responsible and act before the next massacre.

9

Bullying Is on the Rise

Peg Tyre

Peg Tyre is a nationally recognized writer and lecturer on education. She is the author of The Good School: How Smart Parents Get Their Kids the Education They Deserve *and* The Trouble with Boys: A Surprising Report Card on Our Sons, Their Problems at School and What Parents & Educators Must Do.

With a rise in bullying incidents reported in the media across the country, parents and educators are concerned about the amount of unreported bullying that lies beneath the media's radar and the effects that bullying has on its victims. Researchers have learned that the bullies are no longer just the physically intimidating kids, but the popular, academically successful kids who are trying to gain higher social status. Parents, educators, and legislators all need to work together to find comprehensive solutions to the problem.

When Jill Jones sent her 10-year-old, Kacey, off to school in Lewisboro, New York, she knew it was a big day for her little girl. A reserved, self-conscious child, Kacey was wearing new white capri pants she'd insisted her mother buy. All went well until lunchtime, when the fifth-grader sat at a table with some popular girls. "Kacey knew them and liked them but didn't feel like she was in their inner circle," says Jill, 51. Things didn't go as Kacey had hoped. The girls were openly hostile; then, suddenly, one of them dumped ketchup on her

Peg Tyre, "Too Cruel for School: The Rise of Bullying," *Family Circle*, October 1, 2012.

lap. When Kacey, already thoroughly humiliated, jumped up and tried to wipe it off, the girls laughed and mocked her for "getting her period."

As soon as Kacey came home, recalls Jill, "I knew something was wrong, but she didn't want to talk about it." After a few probing questions, the whole story spilled out. "When I realized Kacey had been bullied, I was furious," says Jill, "Then I wondered if I was overreacting. But when I saw how traumatized Kacey was, I knew the incident had crossed the line." Jill realized she needed to take action. "I had to find the best way to intervene so it wouldn't happen again," she says.

Researchers have found that kids are particularly sensitive to intimidation and emotional cruelty.

The Bullying Epidemic

School bullying has many parents worried, and not just those whose kids have been on the receiving end. A series of shocking incidents has garnered headlines and provoked outrage and soul-searching in communities across the country. In Columbus, Indiana, a 13-year-old was charged with felony intimidation after he held a knife against a fellow student's throat in a classroom while the teacher's back was turned. In Yorktown, Virginia, 16-year-old Christian Taylor took his own life shortly after his mother, Alise Williams, complained to high school officials that her son had suffered months of relentless bullying by classmates, including one student who she says told Christian to "just go ahead and commit suicide and get it over with." And in South Hadley, Massachusetts, 15-year-old Phoebe Prince hanged herself early this year [2012] after reportedly being tormented by classmates who called her "Irish whore" and "stupid slut" and sent cruel texts and messages—even after her death. Six teens are now facing charges in that case, ranging from harassment and stalking to violation of civil rights with bodily injury.

Those cases have prompted parents and school officials to ask whether we're just seeing the tip of the iceberg, since bullying often takes place off the radar screen of grown-ups. While overall incidents of school violence, such as assault and theft, have declined in the last decade, bullying is on the rise. Just ask our kids. According to a 2009 federal survey of school crime and safety, 32 percent of middle and high school students said they'd been victimized during the academic year, compared with 14 percent in 2001. Among that group, 21 percent had been made fun of; 11 percent were pushed, tripped or spit on; and 6 percent were threatened.

But is any of that really worse than the verbal jabs, social slights and hard shoves today's parents endured while they were growing up? Most kids tease others and are teased from time to time; it's part of the harmless rough-and-tumble environment at all schools. Bullies, on the other hand, tend to target victims and subject them to repeated abuse. There is frequently a striking power imbalance between perpetrator and prey, whether it's a matter of age, size, academic achievement, popularity or economic status. This more virulent type of harassment has become all too common, according to experts. "The amount of bullying in schools is unprecedented," says Marlene Snyder, PhD, director of development at the Olweus Bullying Prevention Program at Clemson University in South Carolina. "The public is becoming aware of how serious it can be."

Indeed, researchers have found that kids are particularly sensitive to intimidation and emotional cruelty. It makes them feel more fearful and anxious than if they were the victims of theft or a physical attack. And the suffering goes far beyond momentary humiliation. They are more likely to be distracted from learning, get poorer grades and become victims of violent crime. "They feel powerless," says Snyder, "and lose faith in the ability of adults to help them."

Legislators are recognizing that schools and communities need help to deal more effectively with the problem. Last spring Massachusetts Governor Deval Patrick signed a bill that requires teachers to report incidents of bullying, and principals to investigate them. Forty-three other states now have laws against bullying and student-to-student intimidation, whether it takes place in the classroom or hallway, or on the playing field. The Department of Education recently unveiled the Safe and Supportive Schools grants, a $27 million discretionary fund for states to use to create in-school programs to prevent harassment and violence. Parents also need to be part of the solution. Learn what the experts have to say about who's hurting whom, the reasons why, and the steps you can take to keep your kids safe from harm.

The growing frequency and intensity of bullying may be the result of a troubling decline in social skills among adolescents.

Causes for the Increase

Peer abuse has always existed at school, but the kinds of kids who are harassing others have changed. The stereotype of yesteryear—a physically intimidating, low-achieving, socially maladjusted loner—no longer applies. Instead, bullies these days are, often as not, popular kids and academic achievers. "They are alpha girls and quarterbacks and not necessarily kids struggling to gain a social foothold," says Elizabeth Englander, director of the Massachusetts Aggression Reduction Center at Bridgewater State College, which runs anti-bullying programs in K-12 schools. Girls are slightly more likely than boys to act out against others—not physically, but by using tactics like alienation, ostracism and deliberate rumors calculated to inflict maximum psychological damage.

So what causes a student who is doing well to go out of his or her way to hurt another? For one, there's the momentary rush kids get from being perceived as dominant in a group situation. But research suggests that the growing frequency and intensity of bullying may be the result of a troubling decline in social skills among adolescents. In a 2009 study, researchers asked teachers whether they thought children's ability to get along with one another and resolve disputes had improved over the last decade, stayed about the same, declined slightly, or declined significantly. Their response was overwhelmingly negative: 75 percent of educators perceived a significant drop and 25 percent said they saw a slight decline.

Psychologists say that these changes may be connected to the way we're raising our kids. In the last 20 years opportunities for preschoolers and elementary school kids to engage in free play with other children have pretty much evaporated. Instead, parents relentlessly cram their kids' schedules with an array of adult-led academic and sports enrichment activities. While those certainly have their upside, unsupervised interaction teaches young kids impulse control and enhances emotional stability, which in turn helps them manage friendships and other relationships. "In our enthusiasm to make our children smarter and stronger, we've forgotten that they need time and opportunities to learn how to be competent social beings, which is every bit as important as knowing algebra and grammar," says Kathy Hirsh-Pasek, a professor of psychology at Philadelphia's Temple University who has researched and written extensively on the social, cognitive and emotional growth that accompanies play. While there is no direct evidence to suggest that enrolling your kid in pee-wee soccer or conversational Mandarin will increase the likelihood that he'll turn out to be a bully, research indicates that free play—and plenty of it—does indeed enhance skills needed to avoid the aggressor/victim dynamic.

Technology is short-changing our kids as well. According to a 2010 study by the Kaiser Family Foundation, children between the ages of 8 and 18 now spend about 7.5 hours a day tethered to smart phones, laptops or other devices, up from about 6 hours in 2005. And that doesn't include the 1 1/2 hours they spend texting or talking. It adds up to 63 hours of media every week—and it comes at a price, says Gary Small, a neuroscientist at the University of California, Los Angeles, and author of *iBrain: Surviving the Technological Alteration of the Modern Mind* (Harper). "The time young people spend engaged with technology is time not spent playing on the playground, or learning verbal cues and face-to-face skills, like maintaining eye contact," he says. "Those are all things that could help reduce the surge in school bullying."

As teachers and administrators can tell you, creating a safe environment for students isn't easy.

Finding Solutions

Like Jill Jones, parents across the nation are uncertain about how to deal with bullying. Experts say the worst thing adults can do is to ignore it. "There's a common—and very mistaken—belief that it's okay," says Julie Hertzog, director of the Bullying Prevention Project at Pacer, a Minneapolis-based organization for children with disabilities. "Adults say things like, 'It's a normal part of childhood' or 'Boys will be boys,' but that's just plain wrong. And it's not only the targets who suffer. Kids who witness bullying are uncomfortable as well. They often want to help but don't know how to—and fear they could be next."

But as teachers and administrators can tell you, creating a safe environment for students isn't easy. One of the oldest and most respected bullying prevention programs used by K-12 schools across the country is Olweus, which focuses on improving peer relations by identifying and dismantling the group interaction that gives rise to abuse. Research has found that when onlookers provide an audience for bullying by standing around, watching or laughing, they unwittingly encourage and prolong the behavior. The Olweus program, which includes teacher training and community outreach, tries to curb bullying by discouraging "hangers on" from participating. "We help kids recognize that when there is an incident everyone who is involved—or even aware of it—plays a role," says Marlene Snyder of Olweus, who conducts training sessions for teachers to help kids stop bullying as it happens. "Some kids are disengaged onlookers, others know better but enjoy watching, and some egg the bully on. We teach them that the best way to defend others is not to give your power to someone who wants to harm others." Olweus, which costs about $1,500, is paid for by school districts, parent groups, federal grants or private foundations. Many consider it a worthy investment, including schools in California and Virginia, which saw an average 15 percent decrease in bullying after one year.

But even the best of such programs are no silver bullet. In a study published this year, longtime bullying researchers Susan Swearer and Dorothy Espelage found that the most effective interventions are "whole school" approaches that include establishing rules and consequences for bullying, teacher involvement, conflict resolution strategies, classroom curriculum and individual social skills training. "All parts of the school should be brought into the conversation," says Swearer. "What's more, special attention and training must be given to some perpetrators to help them come up with socially acceptable ways of dealing with peers." But none of the programs she and Espelage studied really snuffed out abuse; while one-third of them improved kids' level of knowledge, attitude and perceptions about bullying, they did not reduce the number of incidents. Even more disheartening, some remedies—like the assembly-type program that encourages children to write down the names of aggressors and hand slips of papers to the teacher—can actually contribute to a climate of shaming and blaming that fosters bullying.

Some experts believe it takes even more of a village to curb cruelty and that students should participate in setting limits. Sam Chaltain, author of *American Schools: The Art of Creating a Democratic Learning Community*, believes that bullying is a sign that young people—even high-achieving ones—feel invisible, unconnected and unsure about how to act appropriately. "Like any democratic environment, a school community should have civic ground rules that govern personal behavior. That will help kids understand what is acceptable to say and do so they can become their own anti-bullying program."

Fortunately for Jill Jones, Kacey's elementary school made the right moves. "Her grade had already been organized into teams, so I called the teacher who was her team leader and related what had happened in the cafeteria," Jill says. "This man was not only an excellent instructor but also a supersensitive dad of four kids. He was outraged." The teacher called an emergency meeting of the team leaders, who met with each of the girls involved and laid down the law. They would be suspended if they picked on Kacey again, conspired against her in any way or were even caught talking about the incident. "Believe it or not, the bullies were duly chastened and never seemed to hold it against my daughter," says Jill. Kacey is now a thriving student with plenty of friends. "She's lucky because the teachers at her school embodied the social lessons that they were teaching," says Jill. In other words, they walked the talk. And that made all the difference.

10

Studies Show Cyberbullying Concerns Have Been Overstated

Sharon Jayson

Sharon Jayson has worked in radio, television, and newspapers throughout Texas and has covered behavior and relationships for USA Today *since 2005.*

An increase of media reports of cyberbullying have led people to believe that online interaction is more dangerous for children and teens than it really is. These reports undermine the fact that most bullying of students occurs in face-to-face interactions, not online. The focus on cyberbullying should not distract leaders and parents from solving the problem of traditional bullying.

Orlando—Old-style face-to-face bullying is still the way most young people are victimized, even though it's cyberbullying that seems to get all the headlines, an international bullying expert told psychology professionals Saturday.

Reports of a cyberbullying explosion over the past few years because of increasing use of mobile devices have been greatly exaggerated, says psychologist Dan Olweus of the University of Bergen in Bergen, Norway. He says his latest research, published this spring in the *European Journal of Developmental Psychology*, finds not many students report being bullied online at all.

Sharon Jayson, "Studies Show Cyberbullying Concerns Have Been Overstated," *USA Today*, August 2, 2012. From USA Today - (Academic Permission), August 2, 2012.

"Contradicting these claims, it turns out that cyberbullying, when studied in proper context, is a low-prevalence phenomenon, which has not increased over time and has not created many 'new' victims and bullies," the study finds.

Olweus says his research includes large-scale studies lasting four to five years; one includes 450,490 students in 1,349 schools in grades 3–12 conducted between 2007–10. Another study followed 9,000 students in grades 4–10 in 41 schools in Oslo from 2006–10.

"There is very little scientific support to show that cyberbullying has increased over the past five to six years, and this form of bullying is actually a less frequent phenomenon," he says.

In the U.S. sample, 18% of students said they had been verbally bullied, while about 5% said they had been cyberbullied. About 10% said they had bullied others verbally and 3% said they had bullied others electronically. In the Norwegian sample, 11% of students reported being verbally bullied; 4% reported being the victim; 4% said they had verbally bullied others; and 1% said they had cyberbullied.

Other research about cyberbullying . . . found less of a prevalence than many believe, largely because the studies haven't been uniform in their methods.

His research also finds that 80%-90% of cyberbullied youth were also bullied verbally or physically in-person. Most cyberbullies—who spread false, embarrassing or hostile information online about a peer—also bullied in the traditional ways, he says.

Those who are bullied in any fashion often suffer from depression, poor self-esteem and anxiety and even have suicidal thoughts, Olweus says.

Other research about cyberbullying presented earlier at the American Psychological Association meeting also found less of a prevalence than many believe, largely because the studies haven't been uniform in their methods, experts say.

Findings "vary dramatically," says Ian Rivers, a professor of human development at Brunei University in London. He says there have been many studies about cyberbullying, going back to the early 2000s, but "the one thing that is apparent is we weren't all looking at the same thing."

Two new, unpublished nationally representative studies do offer something more concrete. Researcher Michele Ybarra of the non-profit Center for Innovative Public Health Research in San Clemente, Calif., has found that about 17% said they've been bullied on the Internet in the past year; 83% said they had not. One study was of 1,158 youths and the other of 3,777 adolescents.

Ybarra has also studied whether the bully was perceived to have more power than the victim—redefined as being "bigger than you, had more friends, was more popular, or had more power than you in another way." That power issue does make a difference, her study finds.

"What we see is that those who say they were bullied by somebody with differential power were twice as likely to say they were really upset by it," Ybarra says. "If bullied by somebody with more power than them, they report greater impact on their lives as the result."

Psychologist Dorothy Espelage, of the University of Illinois-Urbana-Champaign, has been studying bullying for 18 years, including the old-fashioned face-to-face bullying and the online variety. She says her research about cyberbullying found the same 17% figure.

Espelage presented a study forthcoming in the journal *Psychology of Violence*, showing that parental monitoring makes a real difference in whether kids bully. Focusing on 1,023 middle school students in the Midwest, she found that "you should probably monitor your kids."

"They may be less likely to engage in perpetration in school and in perpetration online," Espelage says. "We know in criminology and sociology, the No. 1 predictor of any involvement in at-risk behavior is parental monitoring. It seems to be showing up confirmed in the face-to-face (bullying) and seems to be important in the online context."

Another study she co-authored that was also presented at the meeting found that those who are victimized are more likely to be perpetrators themselves. The researchers found that kids who were victimized face-to-face by peers at school were more likely to go online and engage in cyberbullying, to retaliate against what was happening at school.

Olweus, who has studied bullying for decades, says even though cyberbullying is getting a lot of attention, schools and parents should put the focus on countering traditional bullying.

11

Modern Children Have Less Empathy

Darcia Narvaez

Darcia Narvaez is a researcher in the department of psychology at the University of Notre Dame and author of the blog "Moral Landscapes" for Psychology Today. *For more information on the topic below, please see this book: D. Narvaez, J. Panksepp, A. Schore, and T. Gleason, eds.,* Evolution, Early Experience and Human Development: From Research to Practice and Policy. *New York: Oxford University Press, 2013.*

There needs to be a reexamination of the way children are raised in the United States. The country ranks low among developed nations in child well-being due in large part to its departure from the more community-minded child rearing of the past. This makes it difficult for children to develop a strong moral sense, and it leads to behavior difficulties, anxiety, and depression later in life.

Charles Darwin [British scientist and originator of the biological theory of evolution] had high hopes for humanity. He pointed to the unique way that human evolution was driven in part by a "moral sense." Its key evolutionary features are the social instincts, taking pleasure in the company of others, and feeling sympathy for fellow humans. It was promoted by intellectual abilities, such as memory for the past and the ability to contrast one's desires with the intentions of others, leading to conscience development, and, after language acquisition, concern for the opinion of others and the community at large.

The Decline of Children's Moral Sense in the United States

Darwin's "moral sense" is often interpreted as if these characteristics are universal among human beings. But empirical research demonstrates how early experience and caregiver-child relationships influence the development of community-minded maturation. Our work shows that the roots of moral functioning form early in life, in infancy, and depend on the affective quality of family and community support. Today, child rearing practices and family supports (or lack of) in the U.S. are undermining the development of the moral sense.

As indexed by a recent UNICEF [United Nations Children's Fund] study of child well-being in 21 rich countries that ranked the USA 20th in family and peer relationships and 21st in health and safety, by the growth of childhood problems, and by the burgeoning prison population, American culture may be deviating increasingly from traditional social practices that emerged in our ancestral "environment of evolutionary adaptedness" (EEA). Empathy, the backbone of compassionate moral behavior, is decreasing among college students.

The way we raise our children it seems that the USA is increasingly depriving them of the practices that lead to well being and a moral sense.

Anthropologists, who have documented early life for young children in foraging communities (representing the EEA where the human genus is presumed to have spent 99% of its existence) note that "young children in foraging cultures are:

- "nursed frequently;
- held, touched, or kept near others almost constantly;

- frequently cared for by individuals [adults] other than their mothers (fathers and grandmothers, in particular) though seldom by older siblings;
- experience prompt responses to their fusses and cries;
- and enjoy multiage [free] play groups in early childhood."
- along with natural childbirth
- and 2–5 years of breastfeeding.

My laboratory and others are documenting the effects of these practices on child outcomes and finding relations to intelligence, cooperation, conscience, empathy, self-control, aggression and depression.

In fact, the way we raise our children it seems that the USA is increasingly depriving them of the practices that lead to well being and a moral sense.

We have among the worst mother and infant mortality in the world, in part because the obstetric system is geared toward efficiency as opposed to concerns for child well-being.

Breastfeeding is too frequently discouraged by a medical system that routinely interferes with the establishment of breastfeeding in the first days of life.

Based largely on unfounded fears and extreme cases, parents are encouraged to sleep apart from their infants who often have limited physical contact with caregivers during the day.

Many parents believe that letting a baby cry is compatible with adequate parenting (it's not).

Instead of shared care giving by extended family members, as was typical for our species, many children spend their early years in emotionally suboptimal daycare facilities, with little individualized, responsive care.

Centers and schools typically separate children into same-age groups where they are seldom allowed to play freely with each other in the natural world, interfering with healthy development of both body and brain.

We can now map the sub-optimal consequences that arise from sub-optimal care.

Formula fed infants have worse outcomes on every front that has been examined.

Lack of touch and social support have detrimental effects on children's growth and development.

Too many children are arriving at school with poor social skills, poor emotion regulation, and habits that do not promote prosocial behaviors or life success.

Regular caregiver neglect through non-responsiveness to infant fusses and cries, perhaps due to overstressed parents or daycare workers, promotes the development of a stressed brain that is detrimental to physical, social and moral outcomes.

Free play, once a hallmark of childhood is now becoming scarce, despite recent findings that it is critical for maintaining mental health, developing intelligence and a fully social brain.

The Effect of Modern Child Rearing

These are just the tip of the iceberg. It is becoming increasingly clear that the ways we are rearing our children today are not the ways humans are designed to thrive. As [author] Thomas Lewis and colleagues point out: "A good deal of modern American culture is an extended experiment in the effects of depriving people of what they crave most."

The ill effects of these missing ancestral practices are becoming evident as children's well being is worse than 50 years ago. Characteristics that used to be limited to a subset of the population from neglect and abuse are becoming mainstream. Too many children are arriving at school with poor social skills, poor emotion regulation, and habits that do not promote prosocial behaviors or life success.

- The USA has epidemics of anxiety and depression among the young, indeed all age groups, and these are real numbers not artifacts of increased diagnosis.
- Rates of young children whose behavior displays aggression, delinquency, or hyperactivity are estimated to be as high as 25%.
- The expulsion rate of prekindergarten children and the number of children under age 5 with psychosocial problems or on psychotropic medications have increased dramatically.
- Ten years ago, it was determined that one of four teenagers was at risk for a poor life outcome and trends have not improved.

Although we can continue to minimize these problems and the risks in childrearing we are taking, the negative trajectories in well-being among children in the USA suggest that a reexamination of our cultural practices is needed. To the extent that our kids are not fully functioning threads in the social fabric, the quality of our cultural moral fiber is diminishing.

What Darwin considered the moral-engine of positive human thriving may be under threat. Ill-advised practices and beliefs have become normalized without much fanfare, such as the common use of infant formula, the isolation of infants in their own rooms, the belief that responding too quickly to a fussing baby is spoiling it, the placing of infants in impersonal daycare, and so on. We recommend that scientists and citizens step back from and reexamine these common culturally accepted practices and pay attention to potential life-time effects on people. It is an ethical issue.

Don't blame mothers. Before the last decades, mothers were never alone in raising children, they always had the extended family and friends on a daily basis. The responsibility for child rearing belongs to the whole community in how it sets up neighborhoods (e.g., is it easy for children to play outside in nature), workplace life (is there daycare where moms can nurse), policies that support families (like paid parental leave after a child is born), and school practices (is there frequent recess). We can change our culture again to support children and families. Perhaps the greatest challenge is that many of us were raised in less-than-ideal conditions and we think we turned out just fine. We are the frogs in the pot that started out in cold water. Now that the water is hot, we can't jump out.

12

Younger Generations Are More Accepting of Others

Thom S. Rainer and Jess W. Rainer

Thom S. Rainer is a pastor, researcher, and the author of over twenty books, including coauthor of Simple Church. *Jess W. Rainer is an assistant pastor and seminary student.*

Growing up during the 1960s made it difficult to avoid developing racist attitudes; however, just twenty years later, racism is already becoming a foreign concept. Generations growing up after the civil rights movement are more open and accepting because that is what they have always experienced. Newer generations are more respectful of elders, accepting of multi-ethnic families and same-sex couples, and place a higher value on marriage. There are many reasons to be optimistic about the next generations.

I (Thom) [Note: This viewpoint is cowritten by father and son, Thom and Jess, comparing their research and experiences growing up in different generations] wish I could say that my life has always been one that showed no prejudices and that never judged a person by the color of his or her skin or ethnic background. But such is not the case.

I grew up in Union Springs, Alabama, a small town in the southeastern part of the state. Union Springs is about twenty miles from Tuskegee, forty-five miles from Montgomery, and

Thom S. Rainer and Jess W. Rainer, "The New Normal of Openness and Diversity," *The Millennials: Connecting to America's Largest Generation*. Nashville, TN: B&H Publishing, 2011.

ninety miles from Selma. Those three towns are historically linked to the Civil Rights Movement and to the world of African Americans in the United States.

In 1964 and 1965 African Americans in Alabama grew frustrated at the systematic denial of blacks to register to vote. Numerous attempts to register resulted in more than three thousand arrests, police violence, and economic retaliation. On March 7, 1965, some six hundred civil rights marchers left Selma heading toward Montgomery to protest their denial of these basic rights. But they traveled only six blocks before reaching the Edmund Pettus Bridge. There state troopers and local sheriff's deputies, who wielded billy clubs and tear gas, attacked the marchers. Many were severely beaten, and all were driven back to Selma.

That day became known as "Bloody Sunday." I was nine years old.

Such was the world where I grew up. I remember my father driving me by Dexter Avenue Baptist Church in Montgomery and telling me about its famous young preacher named Martin Luther King Jr. And though I don't know if it's my recollection or my father's retelling of the story, I have memories of my dad in an argument with our circuit judge named George C. Wallace. Of course, Wallace later became a multiterm governor of Alabama and a candidate for the presidency of the United States. He is most famous for his staunch stands for segregation of races.

It is more likely that I recalled my dad's telling of the story because I was not even six years old. But that is the world that shaped me and influenced me.

In my early years I really didn't think twice about going to segregated schools, or drinking from separate water fountains, or having separate waiting rooms at the doctor's office. That was my world.

But I do remember my uneasiness when integration began in my school when I was in the fifth grade. I remember how strange it seemed to have a black student named Henry Huffman in my class. And I remember trying to be nice to him but never developing a relationship that could truly be called a friendship.

After all, good white boys just didn't do things like that. That was my world.

Racial and ethnic diversity have always been a part of my life. I have known no other world.

Then I remember in my teen years when I began to see the evils of racism and prejudice. And I remember my anger toward the white population of my town, those who had, from my limited view, perpetuated the racism. But that was the world they knew as well.

For these reasons and more, racial and ethnic diversity will always be an issue for me. I made the transition from the acceptance of racism to an advocacy against it. It will always be a conscious part of my world.

A Tale of Two Worlds

His perspective seems so strange to me (Jess). I've heard my dad talk about the Civil Rights Movement and the culture of racism where he grew up. But his stories sound more like a history book than any reality I've known.

One of my first friends was named Femi Babalola. His family moved to the United States from Nigeria. In fact, as I look back to my childhood, racial and ethnic diversity have always been a part of my life. I have known no other world.

I remember Dad asking me if one of my friends was getting married to the Asian girl he was dating. I actually had to pause for a moment to think about his question. When I thought of my friend's fiancé, her ethnic background was not the first thought in my mind.

My generation is not naïve. We know racism still exists. We know that injustices still take place. But our world is so different from the world of the Baby Boomers [generation of people born from 1946 to 1964]. When I read about the racism and the Civil Rights Movement, particularly in the 1960s, it seems so distant. But my father was only a kid in that decade. From 1960 to 1969 his age was five to fourteen. I can understand how all of these events impact him so significantly. I can understand how a boy growing up in south Alabama was shaped by this world.

But it's not the world I know.

My generation hardly ever saw racial and ethnic diversity as an issue; we rather see it as normative. The Millennials [generation of people born from 1980 to 2000] rarely describe someone first by their skin color or by their ethnic origin. That's not what is at the foremost of our minds. For us ethnic diversity is normative. I even struggle with the title of this chapter, "The New Normal of Openness and Diversity." For me this is nothing new. It is the life I've always known.

But from the older coauthor's perspective, it is a new normal. It is a major change from the Baby Boomers to the Millennials.

So I will yield to the perspective of the old man.

A Richly Diverse Generation

The Millennials represent the most racially and ethnically diverse nation in America's history. This is also the generation with the lowest proportion of Caucasians. By 2000 nonwhites and Latinos accounted for more than one-third of the total population of the Millennials. That's nearly 50 percent higher than their representation in the Boomer generation, and nearly *200 percent* higher than that of the seniors born before 1946. The world of the Millennials is indeed different from that of their parents and grandparents. . . .

So how does this generation that was raised in a racially and ethnically diverse world fare today? As one might expect, these young adults are developing relationships in much the same pattern as they were raised.

In our study we asked about the backgrounds of their friends. Did those closer relationships come from people more like you or less like you? The responses were intriguing. About 70 percent of the Millennials acknowledged a friendship with someone of a different ethnic or racial background. From our perspective this response is the true test of crossing barriers. The Boomer generation became the generation of tolerance, but the Millennials do not simply "tolerate" those of different skin colors or ethnic backgrounds. They are far more likely to embrace them as friends and to make them a part of their world.

But we did not limit our questions of openness and diversity to just race or ethnicity; we also asked questions regarding religion, age, and lifestyle. The responses again reflect the ease by which this generation interacts with others who are different from them. The same high number, 70 percent, say they have friends who have different religious beliefs. . . .

---

94 percent of the Millennials indicate that, to some degree, they have great respect for older generations.

We further asked if they had friends who had different lifestyles from their own, and these responses were even higher. Though we didn't define "lifestyle" with specificity, 80 percent of the Millennials affirmed that their circle of friends included those who lived differently from them. Some of the respondents spoke of friends who had a different sexual orientation than their own. Others related the lifestyle issue to wealth or social standing.

Still others said that some of their friends had different lifestyles because of contrasting religious beliefs, an obvious indicator that our questions were not mutually exclusive. "I grew up in a nonreligious family," Todd told us. "But one of my best friends describes himself as a born-again Christian. We are good friends, but we really do have contrasting lifestyles. I guess you could call his lifestyle strict compared to mine."

Another indicator of the diversity of and acceptance by this generation is their relationship with those of other generations. Over three-fourths of the Millennials have a friendship with someone of another generation. Of course, the Millennials are the youngest adult generation in America today, so we can only presume that these friendships are with older people. Indeed some of the other questions affirm our presumptions. Let's look at this issue a bit more closely.

The Attitudes of a More Open Generation

The Millennials simply see many things differently from previous generations. As we indicated earlier, it would be wrong to see their openness as mere tolerance toward others. They have moved beyond tolerance and acceptance to acting upon their beliefs.

Toward older adults. For example, we just mentioned the issue of friendships across generations. In one of the most overwhelming responses of the survey, 94 percent of the Millennials indicate that, to some degree, they have great respect for older generations. This response really caught the two of us by surprise. It may prove to be one of the most significant findings of this study.

I (Thom) remember well when one of the slogans of the Baby Boomer Generation was "Trust no one over thirty." Most of us believed that and lived it, at least until we turned thirty. Now our children are saying that some of their key friendships are with older adults. And they told us that those for whom they have the greatest respect are older adults. What a significant shift between the two largest generations!

But this makes perfect sense to me (Jess). . . . Millennials tend to be close to their Boomer parents. That is certainly how I view my own parents. Many of us have never known a time when we didn't have a close relationship with someone older than us. Yeah, our parents were sometimes "helicopter parents," hovering over us in matters of the smallest details. But we knew that they loved us, that they were looking after our best interests, and that we could talk freely at any time. It is little wonder that today we have a healthy respect for older adults.

We tried to discern a pattern among different subgroups of Millennials, but the only pattern we found was consistency. Respect for older adults crossed gender lines, racial and ethnic lines, and religious lines. No matter where we looked in this generation, we found a healthy respect, if not admiration, for older adults.

But the times are surely changing. And the Millennials are leading the way.

It is indeed a different world.

Toward mixed racial/ethnic marriages. I (Thom) have clear memories of my white cousin marrying an African-American man when I was thirteen years old. It was the scandal of the decade in my hometown. I recall two distinct reactions. The first type of reaction came from the outspoken critics who couldn't stop talking about it. Of course, many of their comments were laced with racist words and phrases. The other reaction came from those who refused to speak about it in any way. It was as if their silence meant that the "problem" did not exist.

I wish I could say that I had no issue with the marriage, but such was not the case. I was highly influenced by the culture of the deep South and residents of my hometown. Unfortunately I still remember anger toward my cousin that she would do such a thing.

But the times are surely changing.

And the Millennials are leading the way. When we asked them if they saw anything wrong with two people of different races or ethnic backgrounds getting married, an overwhelming 93 percent said no!

"I don't get it," said Kevin, a white twenty-four-year-old from Minnesota. "It's just skin color. Why do older people get so upset about it? It just makes no sense to me. Look, I've known many times when two white people marry, they have a ton of trouble. They're not compatible so they get a divorce. Two people with different skin color can have more in common than two with the same skin color."

Again, subgroups of Millennials have the same attitude as the generation as a whole. Mixed marriages by race or ethnicity are simply not a problem for these young adults regardless of gender, race, ethnic background, or religious preferences.

Millennials also expressed a willingness themselves to be married to someone outside their racial or ethnic group. Nearly nine out of ten, 87 percent, expressed this attitude.

Interestingly, when we asked the married Millennials how many of them had actually married outside their racial or ethnic group, only 22 percent said they had done so. Still, nearly one out of four is a high number by historical standards. With the open attitude expressed by the Millennials, we will not be surprised if that number increases in the years ahead.

Toward same-sex marriages. The Millennials are definitely more open to same-sex marriages than predecessor generations. Six out of ten expressed no concern about homosexual marriages, but the number was only four out of ten who were strongly supportive.

This is one of those issues that has significant variation among subgroups. Men, African-Americans, and residents of the South were considerably less comfortable with same-sex marriages than other subgroups.

As one might expect, though, the greatest variation came from religious subgroups of this generation. For example, if the Millennial did not attend church, he or she was in a group where 74 percent are supportive of same-sex marriages. An even higher number, 85 percent, of those who said they have no religious background were in favor of homosexual marriages.

But the numbers decrease dramatically when a Millennial labeled himself or herself "Christian." Barely a majority, the number supporting same-sex marriage drops to 51 percent. . . . [The] self-label of "Christian" applied to those who may have no commitment to historical Christian beliefs, but who say it's the closest religious term for them.

When we began defining Christianity by a series of questions that we labeled the "born-again" group, the number supporting homosexual marriages dropped dramatically again to 26 percent. And when we further defined the Christian faith to basic core doctrinal beliefs, the number in favor of same-sex marriage dropped even more to 16 percent.

At this point we can make two conclusions about the Millennials and their openness to same-sex marriage. First, they are more supportive than any previous generation. Second, the closer one holds to the historical and doctrinal tenets of Christianity, the more he or she would be opposed to homosexual marriages. The culture wars are not yet over on this issue, but those who are open to same-sex marriages have made significant gains with this generation. . . .

Toward multiple marriages. Much has been said about the divorce rate in America, and the number of people who will marry more than once. So how do the Millennials feel about divorce and remarriage? In light of the previous discussion on same-sex marriage, their responses are somewhat surprising. On this issue they actually take a more conservative turn.

Despite the dire marriage statistics this generation faces, the Millennials remain both optimistic and determined to make marriage work. And because of the broken homes they experienced, this generation is committed to making marriage work. . . .

Few Millennials actually believe that they will marry more than once. In fact, the number is overwhelming: 84 percent of this generation believe they will not marry more than one time. A few who responded to our question doubt they will marry at all. But the reality remains that for over eight out of ten Millennials, divorce is not considered an option.

Of course, we understand that belief and action are not always the same, but the attitude to make marriage work in this generation is extremely healthy. Indeed, family is the Millennials' number one priority, including their determination about marriage. . . .

Not necessarily what you expect. The attitudes of the Millennial Generation defy any neat categorization. They are certainly open to diversity among races and ethnic groups. Perhaps it's better to say diversity is normal for them; anything else seems strange.

Likewise, this generation has a great attitude about relationships with older adults. As we [previously] saw . . . , this attitude seems to stem from the overall healthy relationships they have with their parents.

Contrary to the attitudes of their parents in earlier years, this generation does not view older adults with enmity.

It is unlikely that the often-heated discussion about homosexuality and same-sex marriage will go away with this generation. Still, there is a definite shift more open to both with the Millennials. On this particular issue we saw significant variances among the subgroups.

While the issue of sexuality is trending more liberal, the issue of divorce and remarriage is trending more conservative. . . .

Overall a Good Report

Though some will express concern about the Millennials and their views on diversity and openness, the report overall is good. Many will applaud their color blindness toward those of different races and ethnicities. Some will have concerns about the helicopter parents, but most will be pleased that this generation has such healthy relationships with their mothers and fathers.

Most will be gratified that the Millennials as a whole have a commitment to stay in one marriage. Of course, the skeptic will insist on a wait-and-see approach. He or she will not be satisfied with the intentions of this generation.

And there is significant evidence to tell us that the Millennials will cross generational lines with little problems. Contrary to the attitudes of their parents in earlier years, this generation does not view older adults with enmity.

"I'm really glad I'm a part of this generation," Zach said with a smile. "I like how we are the generation that has such great relationships with people who look differently or have another ethnic background. I think we have a real opportunity to make a difference for the good. I think the world could be a better place because of us in twenty to forty years. I say that hopefully and not arrogantly."

Zach represents many in his generation who are really motivated to make a difference.

Organizations to Contact

The editors have compiled the following list of organizations concerned with the issues debated in this book. The descriptions are derived from materials provided by the organizations. All have publications or information available for interested readers. The list was compiled on the date of publication of the present volume; the information provided here may change. Be aware that many organizations take several weeks or longer to respond to inquiries, so allow as much time as possible.

American Academy of Pediatrics (AAP)
141 Northwest Point Blvd., Elk Grove Village, IL 60007-1098
(847) 434-4000 • fax: (847) 434 8000
website: www.aap.org

The mission of the American Academy of Pediatrics is to attain optimal physical, mental, and social health and well-being for all infants, children, adolescents, and young adults. AAP recommendations form the basis of pediatric preventive health care. Their website includes issue policy statements, clinical and technical reports, and practice guidelines on a broad range of topics. AAP also produces a website for parents and caregivers, HealthyChildren.org, that includes guidance on parenting issues and links to AAP news articles.

Center on Media and Child Health (CMCH)
300 Longwood Ave., Boston, MA 02115
(617) 355-2000 • fax: (617) 730-0004
website: http://cmch.tv

The Center on Media and Child Health at Children's Hospital Boston, Harvard Medical School, and Harvard School of Public Health is dedicated to understanding and responding to the effects of media on the physical, mental, and social health of children through research, translation, and education. The mission of CMCH is to conduct, coordinate, and compile scientific research to improve the understanding of how media affect children's health in positive and negative ways and provide evidence-based expertise to initiatives and programs that address children's involvement with media. Their website includes reports from and updates on their research, links to their newsletter, and additional information for parents and teachers on media use and children.

Child Mind Institute
445 Park Ave., New York, NY 10022
(212) 308-3118
website: www.childmind.org

The Child Mind Institute is dedicated to transforming mental health care for children everywhere by finding more effective treatments for childhood psychiatric and learning disorders, building the science of healthy brain development, and empowering children and their families with help, hope, and answers. The institute works to improve the lives of children and teens struggling with psychiatric and learning disorders by integrating clinical care, research, information, resources, and advocacy. Resources available on their website include a symptom checker to help differentiate normal childhood behaviors from those that may need attention, as well as information about the latest treatments and research in child mental health.

Children and Adults with Attention-Deficit/ Hyperactivity Disorder (CHADD)
8181 Professional Place, Suite 150, Landover, MD 20785
(301) 306-7070 • fax: (301) 306-7090
website: www.chadd.org

CHADD is a national organization providing education, advocacy, and support for individuals with attention-deficit/ hyperactivity disorder (ADHD). CHADD provides training for parents and educators and holds an annual conference. The organization publishes a variety of printed materials to keep members and professionals current on research advances, medications, and treatments affecting individuals with ADHD.

These materials include *Attention* magazine; *News From CHADD*, a free electronically-mailed current events newsletter; and other publications of specific interest to educators, professionals, and parents. Many of these resources along with additional information and support for those living with or caring for someone with ADHD are available on the organization's website.

Common Sense Media

650 Townsend, Suite 435, San Francisco, CA 94103
(415) 863-0600 • fax: (415) 863-0601
website: www.commonsensemedia.org

Common Sense Media is dedicated to improving the lives of kids and families by providing trustworthy information to help children thrive in a world of media and technology. The organization conducts research to provide parents, educators, health organizations, and policymakers with reliable, independent data on children's use of media and technology and the impact it has on their physical, emotional, social, and intellectual development. The group's research reports are available on its website along with media reviews and advice for parents and educators.

Council for Children with Behavioral Disorders (CCBD)

2900 Crystal Dr., Suite 1000, Arlington, VA 22202-3557
(888) 232-7733
website: www.ccbd.net

CCBD was founded in 1997 by the Council for Exceptional Children to support their mission of improving the education of children and youth with emotional or behavior disorders (EBD). The organization provides members of the educational, research, and wider community with a way to combine their efforts though funding projects, programs, and curriculum; providing financial assistance for educators to attend professional development events; and awarding scholarships to students pursuing a career working with students with EBD.

CCBD's website includes information on its annual conference, links to its publications *Behavioral Disorders* and *Beyond Behavior*, and copies of its monthly newsletter and position papers.

Council for Exceptional Children (CEC)
2900 Crystal Dr., Suite 1000, Arlington, VA 22202-3557
(888) 232-7733
website: www.cec.sped.org

The Council for Exceptional Children is the largest international professional organization dedicated to improving the educational success of individuals with disabilities and/or gifts and talents. CEC advocates for appropriate governmental policies, sets professional standards, provides professional development, advocates for individuals with exceptionalities, and helps professionals obtain conditions and resources necessary for effective professional practice. CEC publishes and distributes products designed to help practitioners work more effectively in the classroom, many of which are available on its website. The website also hosts a career center and *Reality 101*, CEC's blog written by and for new special and gifted education teachers.

FamilyDoctor.org
American Academy of Family Physicians
11400 Tomahawk Creek Pkwy., Leawood, KS 66211-2680
(800) 274-2237 • fax: (913) 906-6075
website: http://familydoctor.org

FamilyDoctor.org is a resource of the American Academy of Family Physicians (AAFP). Through FamilyDoctor.org, AAFP provides educational content that focuses on prevention and wellness to help consumers make informed decisions about nutrition, physical activity, emotional health, and prevention of disease. The mission of the website is to provide scientifically accurate information from a family medicine perspective to improve the health of all individuals and communities by empowering patients; educating parents, caretakers, and families; and providing tools to facilitate discussions between patients and family physicians. The website includes a section specifically devoted to childhood behavior and emotions and contains content written specifically to children and teens.

Juvenile Bipolar Research Foundation (JBRF)

550 Ridgewood Rd., Maplewood, NJ 07040
e-mail: info@jbrf.org
website: www.jbrf.org

JBRF actively promotes and supports scientific research focused on the cause of and treatments for bipolar disorder in children. The foundation has organized a consortium of collaborating research groups and individual investigators from a number of medical schools and treatment centers and continues to establish collaborations with researchers from other centers around the world. Its website includes extensive information for families and mental health professionals on the latest diagnostic criteria, clinical research, and treatments, as well as articles addressing the concerns about the diagnosis of juvenile bipolar disorder.

National Center for Juvenile Justice (NCJJ)

3700 S Water St., Suite 200, Pittsburgh, PA 15203
(412) 227-6950 • fax: (412) 227-6955
e-mail: ncjj@ncjfcj.org
website: www.ncjj.org

The National Center for Juvenile Justice is the research division of the National Council of Juvenile and Family Court Judges. The group's mission is to secure effective justice for children and families through research and technical assistance. The center prides itself on providing practitioners objective, factual information while maintaining a politically and socially neutral stance. In addition to information on its programs and research, its website includes a searchable database of all NCJJ's publications.

National School Climate Center (NSCC)
341 W 38th St., 9th Floor, New York, NY 10018
(212) 707-8799 • fax: (212) 957-6616
e-mail: info@schoolclimate.org
website: www.schoolclimate.org

The goal of NSCC is to promote a positive and sustained school climate: a safe, supportive environment that nurtures social, emotional, ethical, and academic skills. NSCC helps schools integrate crucial social and emotional learning with academic instruction to enhance student performance, prevent drop outs, reduce physical violence, bullying, and develop healthy and positively engaged adults by translating research into practice. NSCC offers a variety of professional development programs and services to support K-12 schools, after-school settings, educators, parent advocate groups, and states to support sustained school climate improvement efforts. Its website includes copies of its newsletter, reports, and toolkits for schools.

Bibliography

Books

Joseph Allen and Claudia Worrell Allen	*Escaping the Endless Adolescence: How We Can Help Our Teenagers Grow Up Before They Grow Old.* New York: Ballantine Books, 2009.
Mark Bauerlein	*The Dumbest Generation: How the Digital Age Stupefies Young Americans and Jeopardizes Our Future (Or, Don't Trust Anyone Under 30).* New York: Tarcher, 2009.
Pamela Druckerman	*Bringing Up Bébé: One American Mother Discovers the Wisdom of French Parenting.* New York: Penguin Press, 2012.
Tim Elmore	*Artificial Maturity: Helping Kids Meet the Challenge of Becoming Authentic Adults.* Hoboken, NJ: Jossey-Bass, 2012.
Tim Elmore	*Generation iY: Our Last Chance to Save Their Future.* Atlanta, GA: Poet Gardener Publishing, 2010.
Meagan Johnson and Larry Johnson	*Generations, Inc.: From Boomers to Linksters—Managing the Friction Between Generations at Work.* New York: AMACOM, 2010.

Stuart L. Kaplan — *Your Child Does Not Have Bipolar Disorder: How Bad Science and Good Public Relations Created the Diagnosis*. Santa Barbara, CA: Praeger, 2011.

Lynne C. Lancaster and David Stillman — *The M-Factor: How the Millennial Generation Is Rocking the Workplace*. New York: HarperBusiness, 2010.

Madeline Levine — *The Price of Privilege: How Parental Pressure and Material Advantage Are Creating a Generation of Disconnected and Unhappy Kids*. New York: Harper Perennial, 2008.

John Rosemond — *Parent-Babble: How Parents Can Recover from Fifty Years of Bad Expert Advice*. Kansas City, MO: Andrews McMeel Publishing, 2012.

Heather Shumaker — *It's OK Not to Share and Other Renegade Rules for Raising Competent and Compassionate Kids*. New York: Tarcher, 2012.

Paul Tough — *How Children Succeed: Grit, Curiosity, and the Hidden Power of Character*. New York: Houghton Mifflin Harcourt, 2012.

Bruce Tulgan — *Not Everyone Gets a Trophy: How to Manage Generation Y*. Hoboken, NJ: Jossey-Bass, 2009.

Jean M. Twenge *Generation Me: Why Today's Young Americans Are More Confident, Assertive, Entitled—and More Miserable than Ever Before*. New York: Free Press, 2007.

Periodicals and Internet Sources

Anushka Asthana "Child Violence Against Parents on Rise," *The Observer*, October 30, 2010.

Sharon Begley "But I Did Everything Right!," *Newsweek*, August 25, 2008.

Kenneth Board "Too Many Kids Lack Social Graces," *Rockford Register Star*, February 21, 2013. www.rrstar.com.

Po Bronson and Ashley Merryman "Why Can Some Kids Handle Pressure While Others Fall Apart?," *New York Times*, February 6, 2013.

Bryan Caplan "Twin Lessons: Have More Kids, Pay Less Attention to Them," *Wall Street Journal* blog, April 11, 2011. http://blogs.wsj.com.

Jennifer Corbett Dooren "Teen Smoking Keeps Falling," *Wall Street Journal*, December 19, 2012. http://online.wsj.com.

David French "Effort Shock and Parents These Days," *The National Review*, February 20, 2012. www.nationalreview.com.

Nancy Gibbs "The Growing Backlash Against Overparenting," *Time*, November 30, 2009.

Helen Halpert — "Op-ed: Don't Abandon Disciplined Students," *Seattle Times*, February 14, 2013. http://seattletimes.com.

Ryan Jaslow — "Teen Birth Rates Hit Historic Low in US," *CBS News*, February 11, 2013. www.cbsnews.com.

Beth Kobliner — "Are Your Kids Riding the En-tidal-ment Wave?," *Huffington Post*, February 22, 2013. www.huffingtonpost.com.

John McCormick — "Has Teaching Good Manners to Our Children Become Old-Fashioned?," *Huffington Post*, January, 29, 2013. www.huffingtonpost.com.

Catherine Rampell — "A Generation of Slackers? Not So Much," *New York Times*, May 28, 2011.

Chelynne Renouard — "New Research Shows Day Care and Behavior Problems Not Linked," *Deseret News*, February 6, 2013. www.deseretnews.com.

Bonnie Rochman — "Kids Behaving Badly? Blame It on Mom," *Time*, October 26, 2011.

Rick Seaney — "Babies on Planes: It's War!," *ABC News*, March 16, 2012. http://abcnews.go.com.

Sue Shellenbarger — "Therapy in Preschools: Can It Have Lasting Benefits?," *Wall Street Journal*, September 8, 2009. http://online.wsj.com.

Nancy Shute	"Good Parents, Bad Results; Science Is Providing Proof of Where Mom and Dad Go Wrong," *US News & World Report*, June 23, 2008.
Tracy A. Stanciel	"Bad Kids Should Be Kicked Off Airplanes," Good and Bad Parents blog, June 1, 2012. www.chicagonow.com.
Claire Suddath	"Q&A: Why Children Are Annoying on Airplanes," *Bloomberg Businessweek*, September 28, 2012. www.businessweek.com.
Allison Terry	"Why Teen Drinking and Driving Has Been Cut in Half in Past 20 Years," *Christian Science Monitor*, October 11, 2012. www.csmonitor.com.
Leslie Wade	"Some Types of TV Might Improve Behavior in Kids," Schools of Thought blog, February 18, 2013. http://schoolsofthought.blogs.cnn.com.
Jennifer Seter Wagner	"When Play Turns to Trouble; Many Parents Are Now Wondering: How Much Is Too Much?," *US News & World Report*, May 19, 2008.
Mercedes White	"Spanking Lowers IQ, Fosters Aggression, Depression," *Deseret News*, March 6, 2012. www.deseretnews.com.

Index

D

E

F

G

H

I

J

K

L

M

N

O

P

R

W

Y